COMFORT FOOD with

BINDAS

an INDIAN SOUL

MEHAK KANSAL

murdoch books
London | Sydney

CONTENTS

BINDAS: A FREE SPIRIT　　6

1 **THE ESSENTIALS** *16*

2 **STREET EATS** *24*

3 **BUNS & PAOS** *56*

4 **TRADITIONAL EATS** *76*

5 **GRILLS** *110*

6 **SALADS** *132*

7 **NAANS & FRIENDS** *142*

8 **CHUTNEYS & RAITAS** *154*

9 **DESSERTS & DRINKS** *168*

THANK YOU *184*

INDEX *186*

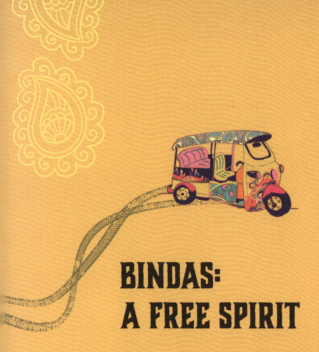

BINDAS: A FREE SPIRIT

Sometimes I look back and feel sheer euphoria and surprise at how I have managed to pour a piece of my heart, travels and happiness into dishes that are being savoured in dining rooms and food halls in London. I had always loved food – food markets, farmers' markets, foraging and growing my own vegetables – but I was not destined to be a cook or restaurateur; I was destined (in the gleaming eyes of my parents) to become a solicitor.

My parents were immigrants. My papa was born in Burma and my mother in Mumbai; her paternal home was in Punjab in North India. They had moved to the UK countryside and settled in the beautiful vastness of Wiltshire. We would often take long walks and bike rides around the village and along the ridgeway. I was out riding horses and quad bikes while others my age were chasing boys and going to the cinema. Every time we passed a newsagent's, I used to race over to the magazines and beg them for a copy of every gardening magazine stacked up on the shelves. I was, of course, refused my request for all magazines, but I was usually provided with one. Each week, the magazine would include a foiled packet of seeds. I would take the seeds, open them up, place them into soil and add water. Often, I was disappointed, as nothing seemed to grow by my hands.

I was about to dig yet another hole in the garden after receiving a packet of radish seeds, but instead – still wearing my wellies and a boiler suit, with a trowel and the packet of seeds in my hand – I found myself taking a detour to our elderly neighbour's house. Her name was Clarice.

She opened the door, giggled at me, and took me through to her garden. I was astonished to see the variety of produce she had grown. Huge vines of loganberries, tomatoes, red currants and runner beans. Ahead of me, I could see pumpkins, potatoes, squash, rhubarb, carrots and lettuce. We went into her greenhouse, and she took out a long planter pot and hauled up a bag of sweet-smelling, dark, moist soil. The soil was placed inside the planter, and then she asked me for the seeds, which I gave her excitedly. I noticed she used the trowel to symmetrically carve out several rows of straight lines. She then placed the seeds neatly within the lines, row by row, until they were all used up. She firmly placed more of the sweet-smelling earth on top of the seeds, almost like she was tucking them in to sleep.

Clarice then gave me strict instructions to pop over once a week to check on their progress. As I was leaving,

she handed me a box of white wild strawberries and told me the best way – the only way – to eat them was on their own.

I had seen these tiny little berries everywhere in Wiltshire, growing freely at the sides of the road, along bridleways and in fields. I opened the box and popped one tiny white leathery jewel into my mouth. It burst, and the taste was uncanny – nothing that I had expected. I had thought it would be watery and fleshy, but I was wrong. Those strawberries tasted like an intense sweet pineapple sherbet, the flavour of which I can still recall to this day. From such an unassuming, unimpressive-looking tiny fruit, a life-changing flavour. I went back every week to check in on my radish plants, and after five weeks, I had the most beautiful fuchsia-coloured radish.

Forgive the pun, but this experience literally sprouted a passion and appreciation for food that would always stay with me.

PORK PIES AND ALOO GOBI

I was that child who ate bangers and mash for lunch and had daal and aloo gobi for dinner. We took packed lunches to school, and I remember being bullied for having a 'smelly' lunch box. My classmates would have cheese-and-pickle or ham sandwiches or pork pies, and mine would be leftover subzi in a sandwich (subzi is the common name for any Indian vegetable dish – aloo gobi, for example). I used to dread opening my lunch box.

One lunchtime, having endured a barrage of bullying the previous day, I placed my lunch box in the bin, walked over to our dinner lady and said my mum had forgotten to give me lunch. She said she had nothing left in the kitchen apart from corned beef sandwiches. I am Hindu, and the consumption of beef is prohibited, but I said that was fine and that I would eat it. I sat alone at the dining table with tears rolling down my face, eating a cold corned beef sandwich.

Having endured this bullying and racism, I became increasingly embarrassed of my heritage. I would not invite friends over, as I would be worried that our home might smell of spices, or that we would be ridiculed for eating roti or chapati with our fingers. Mum would make chicken curry or subzi instead of ordering a pizza. I went through a stage of not appreciating my roots or understanding my culture, as I was trying to fit in and not be 'too Indian'.

FROM NANI WITH LOVE

My nani used to write letters to me once a week. I would look forward to her letters, and would race to the breakfast bar each time I saw that international envelope with blue-and-red dashed lines and big stamped letters saying 'AIR MAIL'. In her letters, she would talk of her beautiful garden, the new mango and lime trees she had planted, and how beautiful her new swings were. She would write about her neighbour Mrs Goel – her arch enemy – and how she would try and pick the best mangoes from Nani's trees. She would write about rogue monkeys that would gorge themselves on her fruit trees, hooting and cackling like naughty children before disappearing over the white

stone wall. Nani would often write about the weather and how the seasons affected her garden and her wardrobe. Every letter always ended with: 'Keep warm, wear your woollens, and I love you. Nanima.'

Almost every weekend, our family would go to friends' and family members' houses for dinner, and the air would be filled with the smells of cumin, onions, ghee, breads and wonderful foods. Papa would indulge in a little red wine or beer. My mother would be so excited seeing hot crispy pakoras and tangy chutneys, deeply rich and spicy lamb curries and layered biriyanis.

My palate had started to develop, and I began to understand there was a delicious world ready to be consumed. When it came to our turn to host, I would ask my mum if she could make more than the few feeble dishes that were always on rotation at home. I am not exaggerating when I say my mother cannot cook; she cannot even be bothered to chop chillies or garlic, and just throws them in whole. Often, I would find myself playing mouth roulette whilst consuming subzi, hoping I wouldn't end up with a mouthful of raw garlic.

I received a rather abrupt answer from my mother, who lovingly told me I had to learn how to cook myself if I wanted to eat anything different. Fortunately for me, my parents ensured that we spent our summer holidays in India with my grandmother so that we could stay rooted in our culture.

That summer – the summer I had decided to seal my culinary fate and surrender to the flavour gods – I was thirteen years old. When we made our annual trip to India, I took a suitcase full of Doritos, Pringles and Walkers crisps for my family there, with the intention of bringing it home filled with spices. We parked up, and as we got out of the car, the humidity and heat hit our faces, and the smell of moisture in the air from the lawn sprinklers hit our noses.

I adored my grandmother's garden. She had a very big lawn full of trees that bore the juiciest sun-yellow kesar mangoes, and fragrant trees bearing little Indian limes and black jamun, which is a small sour plum. I remember peeling away the thick, deep-purple skin to unveil the juicy sweet-and-sour flesh of the fruit. She also grew mooli, carrots, and the largest tomatoes I had ever seen – their skins were such a dark red that they almost looked as if they had been enriched with iron. To the rear of the house there were large vegetable patches. The soil was a chocolate brown, sandy and dry, nothing like the sweet-smelling soil that Clarice used. Inside these crumbly, sandy pits grew cauliflower, potatoes, marrows, turnips, runner beans and chillies. It was a small oasis of bounty.

Nani's harvest had been prepped for pickling. Ahead of us, we saw huge jars of pickles laid out on colourful day beds, facing up towards the blazing sun. I lifted a jar and saw red carrots, yellow turmeric-stained cauliflower, mustard seeds and a dark yellow oily vinegar swirling around the jar. I lifted another packed with green and yellow mangoes, red chillies, fennel seeds, again swirling around in a sweet

and spicy oily vinegar. My mouth had started to water; I was about to taste an Indian summer.

A SUMMER AWAKENING

My grandmother could not cook, but fortunately for us she had the most wonderful cook at home who made fabulous food. The smells seeping from his kitchen were intoxicating. He would make hot, fluffy, puffed-up fried breads known as bhaturas, which he served with a spicy chickpea curry and a homemade turmeric, chilli, ginger and turnip pickle. The thought of this dish brings back some of the fondest memories I have of India.

I dumped my suitcases, had a cold shower, then rushed over to the dining room, where I tore into hot fluffy phulkas and literally inhaled my thali filled with pickles, raita and vegetarian subzis, including my favourite: an aubergine dish called bartha, which is essentially an Indian baba ghanoush (see page 103 for my version). Blistered charred aubergines, mashed flesh, spices, browned onions, tomatoes, garlic, ginger and chillies, all cooked down into this gloriously smoky, spicy, slightly sweet mash. I would use the phulkas as a shovel to scoop up the bartha, then dip it into the raita, before taking a bite of tangy, crunchy, spicy and sweet pickle.

As soon as the sun had gone down, we went to sit on the veranda with Nani, listening to old Bollywood songs and singing 'Qué Será, Será' at the top of our lungs with hot sweet chai in our hands. The air was muggy, and the garden was vibrant and dewy as the sprinklers had been on all day. As we sipped our tea, we could hear the soft chimes gently ring inside the garden temple. The gentle tinkling of the bells, the chirping of crickets, the calls of birds, along with the horns of the autos and shouts of vendors in the streets, created the most unique ambience.

I woke up the next day and showered, and then, eager to learn, I went to the kitchen and pestered the cook to teach me everything. I must have irritated him immensely, but I didn't mind. I wanted to learn, and I asked him what every ingredient was, and what he was doing at every second.

He turned up the heat up on his ferociously hot pans filled with oil, then turned around and shouted, 'CHUP KAR AUR AAP DEHK!' – meaning, 'Be quiet' – and told me to just watch! Sweat was dripping down my face from the heat of the kitchen and the sun, but I did as he said: I stood on a stool right next to him and watched. Mustard seeds, cumin seeds, bay leaves, cinnamon bark, black cardamom and peppercorns hit the pan, the spices foaming and fizzing in the sizzling oil. He threw in a whole bowl of sliced white onions, which began frying and slowly browning in the spicy oil, growing spicy yet sweet as they sweated. The aromatics were being released; the thick air was perfumed. I watched him, imagining him as a maestro conducting an orchestra. I watched meticulously, I smelled intensely and felt deeply.

My nani had a car and driver, and I asked him to take me to the juice market. We were not supposed to go to the juice market, for fear we would get Delhi belly as the fruits were washed

in local water. But it was guava season, and I was prepared to take my chances, so I paid the driver twenty rupees to take me and spent another ten rupees on my juice.

Fortunately, I was safe and Nani was none the wiser, so these little foodie trips to the market became frequent. Next, I wanted to go to the spice market. On the way, our driver stopped to get aloo tikki chaat, and gave me a small banana-leaf plate filled with intoxicating carbohydrate euphoria. Soft potato patties spiced with mustard seeds, curry leaves, turmeric, chilli and coriander, fried until golden, slightly crispy and soft. The tikki was topped with dark chickpea curry, fresh mint chutney, sweet and sour tamarind chutney, sweet and spicy raita, puffed lentils and chopped onions. I didn't know what wizardry it was that I had savoured; all I knew is I wanted food to feel simple yet celebratory like that all the time. I asked the driver to take me to a different street vendor every day. I needed to watch and listen to see how food and drink was prepared. I watched the halwais in the street pour steaming hot chai from a height into short glasses (the significance of pouring chai from a height is that it releases aromatics and develops a creamier texture for the tea). I watched them pull out huge corn on the cobs from piping-hot sandpits, then rub them with lemon, chilli and salt. We ate our way through the markets, restaurants and our cousins' houses throughout the whole of the summer. It was delicious.

With one week to go before bidding adieu to India, I asked Nani to take me to the spice shop, and she kindly obliged. I saw every spice I could imagine. Heaps of colourful powders in yellow, red, brown and green; seeds, chillies, leaves, nuts, whole spices and boxed spices. I bought every packet that I could physically carry and stuffed them all into the now-empty suitcase that I had used to carry all those Doritos.

Returning to the serenity and greenery of the rolling hills of Wiltshire, I walked through the door and unzipped my suitcase, revealing my new treasures to my mum.

She laughed and said, 'You really are going to cook now?'

I replied with a solid and firm, 'Yes, I will.'

I was armed with an array of spices and the mental inventory I'd built while watching the cooks in India. I harvested gooseberries, green apples, carrots, potatoes and radishes. I was going to make a vegetable biriyani with gooseberry pickle and apple chutney.

I spent four hours in the kitchen. I microwaved rice (terrible, I know, but I was thirteen), then fried some onions in a pan with copious amounts of ghee, chillies and garlic, along with cumin seeds, mustard seeds and bay leaves. I then added an array of spices and cooked it all down into a potent masala, to which I then added all my vegetables. Once cooked I took a dish and layered the steamed rice in between my vegetable masala, and served it with apple chutney, plain Greek yoghurt and a quick gooseberry pickle. I served the biryani in my mum's Wedgwood casserole dish, which was decorated with lemons.

BECOMING THE PROVIDER

From that moment on, my fate and affinity for cooking were sealed, and I became the designated cook of the family up until my late twenties. I would cook and bake most weekends. I was asked to bake cakes for most celebrations and taught myself how to make teddy bears and flowers out of fondant.

I went to school in Bath, and every time I would go to a friend's house in Frome, I was asked to make dinner, as my friend and her parents loved my food. I loved making penne arrabbiata and would feel immense joy selecting produce from the local farm shop, and then cooking on a giant Aga armed with beautiful olive-wood spoons, using coarse sea salt, fresh basil and olive oil so dark green in colour it was almost too beautiful to drizzle and consume. I would drive home every Friday evening, and on Saturday morning I would then cook for the whole family, filling up the fridge and packing a few bits to take back to school. I would like to add that this cooking for the family lark carried on until I went to university.

Once at university, I became renowned for my makhani or butter chicken (see page 80); often, I would cook in my halls kitchen, and my friends would gather outside the window asking me what I had prepared and whether I would be willing to part with some of it.

I had started travelling a fair amount, picking up tips, tricks, herbs and spices along the way. As I got older and more experienced, I became passionate about Indian and international food. I wanted to immerse myself in food culture and develop a deep understanding of the heritage of every country I visited. My store cupboard was getting bigger, and my condiment, spice and herb inventory was full to the brim, bursting with possibilities. Cooking and curating dishes became a hobby and a form of therapy for me; it was a chance to express myself.

Meanwhile, I had finished my degree in law and politics and had started working as a paralegal. I hated every minute of it. My training contract fell through as the law firm I was working at was going into administration, so I went from job to job, dissatisfied and unfulfilled, until Papa asked me to move back home and work in the family business. Naturally, I obliged.

I started working with Papa, and I was unsure at one stage of whether he was still my papa or was now a drill sergeant. I did enjoy working in the business, and I was pretty good at it, managing to create some positive uplift, but I craved more responsibility, and I could see that Papa was not ready to let go and let me lead the business.

I had just got married and found myself drowning in work and expectations. I soon fell into a deep depression. I was not able to concentrate in Papa's business, and I was struggling in my role as a wife, daughter-in-law and daughter, as I was contending against oppressive archaic societal norms. My depression made me pull away from all those closest to me, including my family, my friends and my husband. I was suffocating and swimming in a pressure cooker of stress, and I constantly felt that I was inadequate and falling short of my 'duties'. I was never the good traditional Indian girl – but I was Indian, and for the most part of my life, I was good. My culture was an amalgamation of Indian and Hindu values, but ruled by core Western values. It was and still is hard to find a balance between them, but over the years I have managed to find a middle ground and embrace them all.

WELCOME TO BINDAS

I had started a very small food blog, and based on that, I hosted my first supper club, which sold out within days. Soon after, I happened to come across a competition advertised in an online article: a major shopping centre was looking for a food entrepreneur. This food entrepreneur would launch a two-week pop-up and sell their food in the middle of the shopping centre.

I entered – and I won. It was a pinnacle for me; I felt validated, and quickly realised that food, cooking and curating recipes would be my salvation. I knew in that moment I needed to dig into various parts of my soul and find the strength to make this dream come to fruition.

Touching produce, smelling spices and tasting dishes took me to that place of peace and safety I never knew existed, nor realised that my soul craved. Now, I find myself with two eateries in London and more to come; writing this book in God's own country, with a spicy masala chai in my hand and the lingering taste of fiery ginger and sweet jaggery dancing on my tongue and I realise that I was destined to cook.

I love to cook and I love to eat. The cross-pollination style of cooking I will share with you in this book is a pure representation of me. I cook in this way because I want to show the versatility and simplicity of this approach, and to celebrate the ability to layer cultures within a dish. After all, isn't that how cuisine is born? If you look throughout history, you will see how each country has had a non-native herb, spice, fruit, veg or livestock brought over by traders and merchants that has then had a huge impact on their food culture. The cross pollination has already begun. My food and style of cooking is global with an Indian soul. I hope you will love it as much as I do.

THE ESSENTIALS

Before we dive into the recipes, let's look at the ingredients and equipment you'll be using in the rest of the book.

SPICES

Indian food is very varied; it's not about brown slops in a bowl or sugary-sweet, thick, oily curries. It is important to understand that India is made up of 32 states, and each state has its own language and its own dishes. Each state usually draws upon certain spices that become staples in its homes.

Spices are not just for heat. They play an important part in the practice of Ayurveda, a healing tradition with a focus on digestion and keeping the body in harmony. India is an incredibly spiritual place, and as we cook, we pay homage to our roots, our food and our culture. Ayurvedic spices are used to 'balance opposites' as you eat. Try adding more warming spices like cardamom and ginger to your meals when you have a cold. Bitter spices like kasoori methi (dried fenugreek leaves) and turmeric are great if you need more cooling, cleansing notes in your meals. Understanding this will help you to better understand your own spice box or spice cupboard, and the spices you add to your dishes.

CREATING THE ULTIMATE SPICE BOX & HERB SELECTION

There are thousands of spices out there, so it can seem like a daunting task to narrow it down to just a few. Here, I'm sharing my list of spices and herbs for the ultimate spice box or cupboard. You can buy any brand you like, but these are the ones you will use throughout this book. Once you become familiar with them, you will quickly see how versatile they are and how easy it is to use them in your dishes. All the spices listed are widely available in supermarkets or can be found online.

SPICES

WHOLE SPICES

* cumin seeds
* mustard seeds
* ajwain seeds*
* fennel seeds
* cinnamon sticks
* cardamom pods

* *Ajwain seeds, also known as carom seeds or bishop's weed, are very important in Indian cookery. They have a potent bitter and herbal flavour similar to that of thyme. Ajwain seeds are often used to treat fungal and digestive issues.*

GROUND SPICES

* garam masala
* ground turmeric*
* ground cumin
* ground coriander
* chilli powder
* smoked paprika

* *Vibrant yellow turmeric is known for its colour, but it also aids with digestion and has antibacterial properties.*

HERBS

* tarragon
* oregano
* kasoori methi (dried fenugreek leaves)*
* curry leaves
* bay leaves

* *Kasoori methi is made with dried fenugreek leaves that are light green in colour and have a very strong aroma. Fenugreek is that magic spice* that takes the dishes up a notch and inserts a nutty, herby, savoury and slightly bitter flavour.

LAYERING SPICES

Layering spices is an important process when making Indian food. Each spice has a different flavour profile and should be added at different stages of the dish's preparation.

Whole spices, along with bay leaves and curry leaves, are tempered first in the oil so that the aromas and flavours are released, perfuming and flavouring the oil before the main cooking is even begun. This is done carefully and slowly so that the spices don't burn and become bitter; instead, they should sizzle and release.

The next part of the layering is adding and browning the masala bases – usually onions, chilli, garlic and ginger.

Typically, the ground spices go in once the mixture has browned, as otherwise they can burn easily. Many of them have been ground after roasting so the flavours are even more intense.

GARNISHES

Garnishes are not just there to look pretty; their role is to enhance the flavour of the dish and its Ayuverdic properties. For example, dishes steeped in warming spices that heat the body are then garnished with coriander or mint for their cooling properties.

ESSENTIAL TERMS

A **bhaji** is a fritter made with flours and vegetables and fried. **Bhaji** is also a collective term used to describe a vegetable or mixed vegetable dish.

Chaat literally means 'to lick your lips', and describes a range of over 500 varieties of savoury snack that are extremely popular in India. The base of all excellent chaats is to combine sweetness, spiciness, saltiness, crunchiness, freshness, creaminess and bursts of acidity. Chaats can be made with fruits, vegetables and even cooked meat.

Daal may be very familiar to you – it is a dish made of lentils, beans, or peas that have been boiled to a thick, porridge-like consistency. 'Daal' is also the collective term we use when we refer to lentils, beans and peas.

Masala loosely means spices, but it can also mean a spice blend. It is also used to refer to the flavour base of a dish, usually made up of onions, garlic, ginger and chilli.

Saag is a traditional dish made with a base of leafy green vegetables that have been slowly simmered in spices.

THE ESSENTIALS 19

COOKING EQUIPMENT

You probably have most of the vessels and equipment needed for these recipes in your kitchen cupboards already, but if you don't own one, a cast-iron, heavy-bottomed pot is a great investment that can last a lifetime. I also recommend stainless-steel saucepans – these temper spices very well, as do cast-iron pots. I'd also recommend having a rolling pin on hand.

FREEZER STAPLES

In my opinion, the most time-consuming part of Indian cooking is chopping garlic and ginger! Luckily, I have a little tip that will help you to make that part of your meal preparation super simple and easy: prepare them in bulk and freeze them.

I usually go to a local Asian store and buy ready-peeled garlic; this is readily available and is usually sold in bags weighing 500g (1lb 2oz). I buy my ginger in bulk from the same store, in bags of about the same size.

You will need 6–8 ice-cube trays, a blender/chopper, some freezer bags, labels, a chopping board and some space in your freezer. If you are sensitive to the lingering smell of garlic and ginger on your fingers, I would use some food-preparation gloves for this.

Wash the garlic and blitz it in the blender/chopper with 8 tablespoons neutral cooking oil or mild olive oil and 1 teaspoon salt.

Once blended, use a spatula so you can really get every bit of the mixture and transfer it to your ice-cube trays, aiming to put about 1 tablespoon of the purée into each mould.

Wash and peel your ginger and repeat the process above.

Let your ginger and garlic set in the freezer for 24 hours. Once frozen, pop the cubes out of the trays and transfer them into freezer bags. Label them and put them back into the freezer. These cubes of frozen purée will stay fresh for six months and will make cooking an absolute doddle. In my recipes, I have used tablespoon measures for ginger and garlic purées – just use one cube for each tablespoon.

When using the cubes, you can use them directly from frozen when making hot food. If using them for chutneys, raitas or other cold dishes, remove them from the freezer 30 minutes before and let them thaw and soften, or place in a bowl set over a pan of barely simmering water to speed up the thawing process.

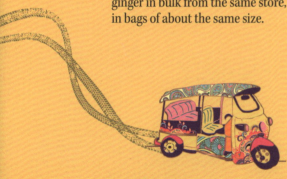

STREET EATS

This chapter offers a tiny snapshot into my travels as well as my heritage. It takes me back to the times I wandered up and down the food markets in Mexico, Malaysia, Türkiye, India, Thailand, Morocco, Italy and many more places, sampling the local street food and learning of new cooking techniques, methods and flavours. Here, I have reworked these dishes to give them an Indian soul.

HOT HUMMUS

SERVES 4

As I moved through the bustle of a busy market in Istanbul, I caught the scent of something warm, toasty, nutty and buttery, mingling with the surrounding aromas of hot charcoal, sizzling meat, Ottoman spices and peppercorns.

I stopped and asked the vendor where the smell was coming from, and he said he was making hot hummus and bread. I stopped to taste it, as I had never eaten hummus warm. It was captivating: the flavour of the tahini, chickpeas and garlic was intensified, and the texture was more condensed. It was nothing like the light, airy versions of hummus I had eaten before. The texture was similar to a warm halwa: dense, comforting and wholesome.

I knew I had to try pairing this warm hummus with Indian spices. At the restaurant, we serve hot hummus with Indian pickling spices and crispy chickpeas roasted in cumin, paprika, turmeric and onion salt. Enjoy it with naans, a dollop of your favourite pickle or chutney, some coriander and a crumbling of feta (optional).

FOR THE ROASTED CHICKPEAS
200g (7oz) canned chickpeas, drained
½ teaspoon cumin seeds
½ teaspoon onion powder
½ teaspoon smoked paprika
1 tablespoon olive oil

FOR THE HUMMUS
350g (12oz) canned chickpeas, drained
4 garlic cloves
4–5 tablespoons tahini
1 teaspoon ground coriander
1 teaspoon garam masala
1 teaspoon smoked paprika
5 tablespoons extra virgin olive oil, plus extra for drizzling
juice of 1 lemon
80ml (2½ fl oz/⅓ cup) cold water
4 ice cubes
1 tablespoon your favourite chutney or pickle, plus extra to serve
sea salt and freshly ground black pepper

FOR THE TOPPINGS (OPTIONAL)
1 tablespoon crumbled feta
a few coriander (cilantro) sprigs
⅓ spring onion (scallion), finely chopped

Preheat the oven to 165°C (320°F/gas mark 2–3) and line a baking tray with baking parchment.

Combine all the ingredients for the roasted chickpeas in the prepared tray and toss to coat well. Roast for 15 minutes until they are lightly crispy on the outside and soft in the middle. Remove from the oven, but leave the oven on.

Add all the hummus ingredients to a blender and blitz to form a smooth paste. Season to taste with a generous pinch of salt and some black pepper, then transfer the hummus into an ovenproof tapas-style dish or bowl. Drizzle with olive oil and place in the oven to heat through for 10 minutes until warm but not piping hot. The surface of the hummus will form a little crust.

Remove from the oven and top with your crispy chickpeas, along with the feta, additional chutney, coriander, spring onion, and anything else you desire! I would recommend you pair this with the Plain Naan on page 144.

TIP *Even though this hummus is served warm, we blend it with ice to make it airier and lighter, and to give it a creamier texture. The beauty of this recipe is that even when you serve the hummus warm, the texture remains fluffy and smooth.*

WATERMELON CHAAT

SERVES 4-6

I made this recipe on a summer's day, when we had some gorgeous sweet watermelon and fancied something that was light, refreshing and packed full of flavour. I chopped up the watermelon, dressed it in chutneys and herbs, and topped it with Bombay mix. I served it with glasses of chilled rosé, and we sat enjoying our view of the countryside.

½ watermelon, cut into 1cm (½in) cubes, seeds removed
handful of mint leaves, chopped
6–7 tablespoons Green Goddess Chutney (page 156)
6–7 tablespoons Grilled Pineapple Chutney (optional) (page 157)
6–7 tablespoons Cucumber & Mint Raita (page 164)

handful of Bombay mix
¼ red onion, finely diced
1 green chilli, finely chopped
2 tablespoons pomegranate seeds
handful of coriander (cilantro), chopped
juice of 1 lime
ground cumin, for dusting
chilli powder, for dusting
sea salt

In a large mixing bowl, combine the watermelon with half of the mint. You will need to work quickly here, as you don't want the watermelon to start releasing all its juices.

Transfer the watermelon and mint mixture to a flat serving dish. Dollop the chutneys and raita over the top in zig-zags or stripes – try to channel your inner Picasso when doing this bit.

Sprinkle over the Bombay mix, onion, chilli, pomegranate seeds and coriander. Squeeze over the lime juice. Season with salt, scatter over the remaining mint leaves and dust with the cumin and chilli powder, then serve.

HAKKA NOODLES

SERVES 4

This dish reminds me of my times spent in the hustle and bustle of Mumbai and Delhi, where you walk through the streets and savour each café's innovative delights. We have a cuisine in India called Indo-Chinese food, and it is very popular in North India and in major cities. Its combinations of sour, sweet, spicy, aromatic and salty are captivating. Hakka noodles are usually made with egg noodles, Indian spices, soy sauce, Chinese aromatics and vinegar. The first time I tried these was at Leopold Café in Mumbai, where they serve their hakka noodles with spring onions, green chillies, green peppers, and roughly sliced cabbage greens.

If, like me, you love to push flavours to the limit and are looking to elevate your humble noodles into something that can be eaten as the main event, then this recipe is for you.

---

4 nests of egg noodles (about 250g/9oz)
2 tablespoons sesame oil (you can use a regular cooking oil if you prefer)
1 teaspoon cumin seeds
1 tablespoon ginger purée
2 tablespoons garlic purée
1–2 green chillies, finely chopped (optional)
1 teaspoon garam masala
1 carrot, peeled and grated
1 red bell pepper (capsicum), finely sliced lengthways
100g (3½oz) tenderstem broccoli (broccolini), roughly chopped
100g (3½oz) spring greens, finely sliced
2 spring onions (scallions), roughly chopped
2 tablespoons tomato ketchup (*secret ingredient – please trust me!*)
2 tablespoons light soy sauce
1 tablespoon rice wine vinegar
sea salt and freshly ground black pepper

FOR THE TOPPINGS (CHOOSE ANY OR ALL OF THE BELOW)
fried eggs with runny yolks (1 egg per person)
1 red chilli, sliced
1 spring onion (scallion), sliced
sesame seeds
crispy chilli oil

Cook the noodles according to the packet instructions, then drain and set aside.

Heat your wok over a medium–high heat. Add the oil and let it get hot, but not too hot or the spices will burn. Add the cumin seeds and let them fizz and pop for 10 seconds, then add the ginger, garlic, green chillies and garam masala. Keep the wok moving and toss the aromatics for 10–20 seconds, then add the vegetables, including the spring onions. Cook for 2 minutes until just softened – take care not to overcook them, as the vegetables need to be a little al dente and not release water.

Add the drained noodles, along with the ketchup, soy sauce and vinegar, and keep tossing until the noodles are completely coated. Season to taste, adding a good pinch of black pepper and some salt if needed.

Garnish your noodles with your chosen toppings – you can even bulk them up by adding prawns, tofu, paneer or chicken to them. Serve and enjoy.

TIP *If you want a sweet-and-spicy-style noodle dish, add 1–2 tablespoons honey/agave at the same time as the noodles.*

STICKY CHICKEN 65

SERVES 4

Chicken 65, one of India's most loved street foods and snacks! This dish originates from Chennai, where it was created in 1965 by a chef who was asked to make a quick snack for guests. It was called 'Chicken 65' after the year of its creation. I have taken the original recipe and added some Indo-Chinese elements, making it sweet, salty, spicy and sticky. Please kindly note this recipe has a 3-hour marination time.

- 600g (1lb 5oz) boneless, skinless chicken breasts, cut into bite-sized chunks
- 2 tablespoons ginger purée
- 2 tablespoons garlic purée
- 1–2 teaspoons chilli powder
- 2 teaspoons ground coriander
- 1½ teaspoons ground cumin
- 1½ teaspoons freshly ground black pepper
- 1½ teaspoons garam masala
- 4 tablespoons Greek-style yoghurt
- 3 teaspoons salt
- vegetable, rapeseed or sunflower oil, for shallow-frying
- 6 tablespoons rice flour
- 6 tablespoons cornflour (cornstarch)

FOR THE STICKY MASALA
- 2 tablespoons sesame or olive oil
- 1 tablespoon cumin seeds
- 2 tablespoons garlic purée
- 2 tablespoons ginger purée
- 20 fresh curry leaves (dried will also suffice)
- 4 green bird's-eye chillies, halved lengthways
- 2 tablespoons tomato paste (concentrated purée)
- 2 tablespoons dark soy sauce
- 1½–3 teaspoons rice wine vinegar
- 2 tablespoons runny honey

TO GARNISH (OPTIONAL)
- sliced spring onions (scallions)
- sliced red chillies

In a large bowl, combine the chicken with the ginger and garlic purées, ground spices, yoghurt and salt. Mix well to coat. Cover and leave to marinate in the refrigerator for at least 3 hours.

When you're ready to cook, pour the oil into a large, shallow frying pan to a depth of 1cm (½in). Heat on the stove over a medium–high heat.

While the oil is heating, add the rice flour and cornflour to the bowl of marinated chicken. Using clean hands, mix it all together so the chicken is coated. It should look dry.

Once the oil is hot, shallow-fry the chicken, working in batches so that you don't overcrowd the pan, as this will make the chicken chewy. Cook the first batch for 4–5 minutes until golden, then flip and cook for 4–5 minutes on the other side. Set aside to drain on a plate lined with paper towels while you fry the rest, then keep warm while you prepare the masala.

To make the masala, heat the oil in a wok over a high heat. Once hot, reduce the heat to medium, then add the cumin seeds and allow to crackle for 10–15 seconds. Add the garlic, ginger, curry leaves and green chillies, then sauté for about 30 seconds until the leaves crisp up a little. Next add the tomato paste and cook for another 2 minutes until the oil rises to the surface.

Add the fried chicken, followed by the soy sauce, vinegar and honey. Toss everything for a minute so that the fried chicken is nicely coated, then taste it and adjust seasoning to taste. If you want more salt, add more soy sauce, and if you want it sweeter, add more honey.

Serve right away, topped with sliced spring onions and chillies.

CHICKEN MANCHURIAN

This is a popular Indo-Chinese dish comprising battered chicken, peppers and minced garlic in a spicy, sticky sauce. If you find sriracha too spicy, you can opt for a sweet chilli sauce instead, or even tomato ketchup.

vegetable, sunflower or rapeseed oil, for deep-frying
600g (1lb 5oz) boneless, skinless chicken breasts, cut into bite-sized pieces
1 tablespoon dark soy sauce
1 teaspoon garlic powder
1 teaspoon garam masala
½ teaspoon chilli powder
1 egg, beaten
2 tablespoons plain (all-purpose) flour
4 tablespoons cornflour (cornstarch)

FOR THE MANCHURIAN SAUCE
1 tablespoon olive oil or sesame oil
1 tablespoon garlic purée
1½ tablespoons ginger purée
1 green chilli, chopped
1 green bell pepper (capsicum), finely chopped
3 spring onions (scallions), chopped
1 teaspoon rice wine vinegar
2 tablespoons tomato ketchup
1 tablespoon dark soy sauce
2 tablespoons sriracha
1½ teaspoons soft light brown sugar
1 teaspoon cornflour (cornstarch)

TO SERVE
1 red chilli, chopped
white sesame seeds
chopped coriander (cilantro)

Pour the oil for deep-frying into a wok or deep pot to a depth of 6–7cm (2½ –2¾ in) and place over a medium–high heat.

While the oil is heating, place the diced chicken in a large bowl and add the soy sauce, spices and beaten egg. Mix well until the chicken is coated. Add the flour and cornflour, and mix again until the chicken is fully coated in the sticky batter.

Test to see if the oil is hot enough for cooking by dropping a little of the batter into the oil. If it crisps up, goes golden and floats, the oil is ready.

Working in batches to avoid overcrowding the pan, add the chicken to the hot oil using tongs. Fry for 4–6 minutes on each side until golden brown and crispy, then carefully transfer to a plate lined with paper towels to drain while you cook the remaining chicken. Keep warm while you prepare the sauce.

To make the sauce, heat the oil in a large frying pan over a medium heat. Add the garlic, ginger, green chilli and green pepper and fry for 1 minute, then add the spring onions and fry for 1 minute more until the spring onions have softened slightly. Stir in the vinegar, ketchup, soy sauce, sriracha and sugar, and reduce the heat to medium–low. Simmer for 1–2 minutes.

In a small bowl, mix together the cornflour and 150ml (5fl oz) water to make a slurry, then add this to the pan. Stir and reduce the heat to low. Simmer for 1 minute until thickened, seasoning to taste.

Add the fried chicken pieces to the sauce and stir until fully coated. Transfer to a serving dish and sprinkle over the red chilli, sesame seeds and coriander to serve.

CHICKEN PAKORAS

Pakoras are fried fritters made with chickpea flour, spices and herbs, bound together with water. You can make them using vegetables, fish or chicken, and enhance the flavours by pairing them with the chutneys in Chapter 8. There is nothing more quintessentially Indian than having chai, chutneys and pakoras.

500g (1lb 2oz) boneless, skinless chicken breasts chopped into bite-sized pieces
1 tablespoon ginger purée
1 tablespoon garlic purée
1–2 green bird's-eye chillies, finely chopped
1 tablespoon cumin seeds
1 teaspoon ground turmeric
1 tablespoon smoked paprika
1 tablespoon dried tarragon
2 teaspoons salt
1 teaspoon freshly ground black pepper
vegetable, sunflower or rapeseed oil, for deep-frying
100g (3½oz) gram flour (also known as chickpea or besan flour)
2 tablespoons cornflour (cornstarch)
¼ teaspoon bicarbonate of soda (baking soda)

TO SERVE
lemon wedges
chopped coriander (cilantro)
Green Goddess Chutney (page 156) or Beetroot Raita (page 163)

Place the chicken pieces in a bowl. Add the ginger and garlic purées, along with the chillies, spices, tarragon and salt and pepper. Mix well and leave to marinate in the refrigerator for 30 minutes.

When you're ready to cook, pour the oil into a wok or large, heavy-based pan to a depth of 7.5cm (3in). Take care not to add too much oil, or it may bubble over. Place over a medium heat.

While the oil is heating up, take the marinated chicken out of the refrigerator. Add the gram flour, cornflour and bicarbonate of soda, and mix well to combine. Now add 180ml (6fl oz/¾ cup) water, a little at a time as you would when making a dough, until the chicken pieces are coated in a thick, velvety batter with a consistency similar to that of thick cream. You may not need all the water.

Test the heat of the oil by dropping a little of the batter into the oil; it should sizzle and crackle, turn golden brown and float to the top.

Carefully add the chicken pieces to the oil using a set of tongs. You will need to work in two batches to ensure the pan isn't overcrowded. Fry the first batch for 4–5 minutes until the coating is golden brown and the chicken is cooked through, then set aside on a plate lined with paper towels to drain while you cook the second batch.

Once all the chicken pakoras are cooked, place in a serving bowl and season with a little sea salt. Serve with lemon wedges, coriander and your chosen chutney!

FISH PAKORAS

SERVES 4-6

500g (1lb 2oz) boneless, skinless white fish (such as haddock), chopped into bite-sized pieces
1 tablespoon ginger purée
1 tablespoon garlic purée
1 teaspoon chilli powder
1 teaspoon garam masala
1 teaspoon ground turmeric
1 teaspoon ajwain seeds
handful of dill, finely chopped
juice of 1 lemon
1 teaspoon salt
1 teaspoon freshly ground black pepper
vegetable, sunflower or rapeseed oil, for deep-frying
100g (3½oz) gram flour (also known as chickpea or besan flour)
2 tablespoons cornflour (cornstarch)
¼ teaspoon bicarbonate of soda (baking soda)

TO SERVE
lemon wedges
chopped coriander (cilantro)
Grilled Pineapple Chutney (page 157) and Mama's Peanut Chutney (page 158)

Place the fish pieces in a bowl. Add the ginger and garlic purées, along with the spices, dill, lemon juice and salt and pepper. Mix well and leave to marinate in the refrigerator for 30 minutes.

When you're ready to cook, pour the oil into a wok or large, heavy-based pan to a depth of 7.5cm (3in). Take care not to add too much oil, or it may bubble over. Place over a medium heat.

While the oil is heating up, take the marinated fish out of the refrigerator. Add the gram flour, cornflour and bicarbonate of soda, and mix well to combine. Now add 180ml (6fl oz/¾ cup) water, a little at a time as you would when making a dough, until the fish pieces are coated in a thick, velvety batter with a consistency similar to that of thick cream. You may not need all the water.

Test the heat of the oil by dropping a little of the batter into the oil; it should sizzle and crackle, turn golden brown and float to the top.

Carefully add the fish pieces to the oil using a set of tongs. You will need to work in two batches to ensure the pan isn't overcrowded. Fry the first batch for 3–4 minutes until the coating is golden brown and the fish is cooked through, then set aside on a plate lined with paper towels to drain while you cook the second batch.

Once all the fish pakoras are cooked, place in a serving bowl and season with a little sea salt. Serve with lemon wedges, coriander and the chutneys.

SPINACH & LEEK PAKORAS

SERVES 4–6

vegetable, sunflower or rapeseed oil, for deep-frying
400g (14oz) baby spinach
2 leeks, thinly sliced

FOR THE BATTER
1 tablespoon ginger purée
1 tablespoon garlic purée
1–2 teaspoons chilli powder
1 teaspoon ground coriander
1 teaspoon ground cumin
1 teaspoon ground turmeric
handful of coriander (cilantro), finely chopped
juice of 1 lemon
1 tablespoon fennel seeds
1 teaspoon salt
100g (3½oz) gram flour (also known as chickpea or besan flour)
2 tablespoons cornflour (cornstarch)
¼ teaspoon bicarbonate of soda (baking soda)

TO SERVE
lemon wedges
chopped coriander (cilantro)
Caramelised Garlic Raita (page 167)

Unlike the Chicken Pakoras on page 34 and the Fish Pakoras opposite, for this recipe, we will make the batter first, then add the spinach and leeks.

Combine all the batter ingredients in a large bowl and mix well to combine.

Pour the oil into a wok or large, heavy-based pan to a depth of 7.5cm (3in). Take care not to add too much oil, or it may bubble over. Place over a medium heat.

While the oil is heating up, start adding 180ml (6fl oz/¾ cup) water to the batter mixture, adding it a little at a time as you would when making a dough. You want the mixture to be thick and velvety, with a consistency similar to that of cake batter or thick cream. You may not need all the water, or you may need a little more. Once you're happy with the consistency, add the spinach and leeks to the bowl and stir well to coat.

Test the heat of the oil by dropping a little of the batter into the oil; it should sizzle and crackle, turn golden brown and float to the top.

Using your hands, take a golf-ball-sized amount of the pakora mix and carefully drop it into the oil, taking care not to splash. Repeat until you have used up about half of the mixture (you will need to work in two batches to ensure the pan isn't overcrowded). Fry the first batch for 3–4 minutes until the coating is golden brown, then set aside on a plate lined with paper towels to drain while you shape and cook the second batch.

Once all the pakoras are cooked, place in a serving bowl and season with a little sea salt. Serve with lemon wedges, coriander and raita.

MASALA POTATO SKINS

This dish has a very special place in my heart, as my family love jacket potatoes and comforting flavours. Here, the acidity from the pickled cabbage cuts through the creamy, cheesy skins. There is the hum of spring onion, a hit of chilli and spice, gooey cheese, cooling soured cream and aromatic herby pesto. Choose between the crunchiness of a peanut chutney or the savouriness of a tomato chutney, all brought together by the sweetness of honey. This recipe combines flavours from India, USA, Germany and England to create the ultimate comfort food.

4 large baking potatoes
1 tablespoon olive oil (if baking)
handful of grated Cheddar (I like to use mature Cheddar for this)
handful of grated mozzarella
sea salt and freshly ground black pepper (if baking)

FOR THE FILLING

2 spring onions (scallions), finely chopped
2 green chillies, finely chopped
1 teaspoon chaat masala (if you cannot get hold of this, a splash of lemon juice will do)
2 tablespoons chopped coriander (cilantro)
2 tablespoons finely chopped chives
1 teaspoon ground cumin
1 teaspoon ground coriander
1 teaspoon chilli flakes
1 teaspoon ground turmeric
3 tablespoons full-fat cream cheese

TO SERVE

1 tablespoon Chilli Garlic Pesto (page 161)
1 tablespoon Mama's Peanut Chutney (page 158) or Nanima's Tomato Chutney (page 160)
1 tablespoon soured cream
1 tablespoon pickled red cabbage (shop-bought)
drizzle of runny honey
2–3 spring onions (scallions), finely chopped
pinch of sea salt (if needed)

You can oven-bake or microwave the potatoes. I would recommend you bake them, if you have the patience.

To bake, preheat the oven to 200°C (400°F/gas mark 6), rub each potato with the olive oil, and season with sea salt and cracked black pepper. Individually wrap in foil and bake for 1 hour.

To microwave, pierce each potato several times with a fork and place on a microwave-safe plate. Microwave on high for 10–12 minutes.

Once the potatoes are cooked through, allow them to cool completely.

In a mixing bowl, combine all the filling ingredients and mix well to combine.

Preheat the oven to 180°C (350°F/gas mark 4).

Halve the cooled potatoes lengthways. Use a spoon to scoop out the flesh from the middles, leaving enough at the sides for the potatoes to keep their shape. Add the potato flesh to the mixing bowl with the filling ingredients and use a fork to mix and mash the ingredients together. Taste and season with more salt and pepper if needed.

Arrange the potato-skin shells on a baking tray and carefully fill each one with the filling mixture. Once filled, top with the grated Cheddar and mozzarella. Bake in the oven for 5–10 minutes until the cheese has melted and turned bubbly and golden brown.

Once cooked, place the stuffed skins on a serving tray. Dollop over the pesto, your chosen chutney and the soured cream. Add little mounds of pickled cabbage, drizzle over the honey and scatter over the spring onion. Season with a little salt if needed, and serve.

SWEET POTATO CHAAT

SERVES 4–6

This, I am sure, is going to become a staple in your home whenever you feel like having a refreshing, zingy, summery dish. It turns a humble veggie into a showstopper. Here, I've used the Green Goddess Chutney and the Apple Raita from Chapter 8, but any chutney would work, as long as you are adding sweet, savoury and spicy notes to your dish.

3–4 sweet potatoes
drizzle of olive oil
1 teaspoon cumin seeds
1 teaspoon fennel seeds
1 tablespoon dried tarragon
1 teaspoon smoked paprika
1 teaspoon chaat masala
1 teaspoon salt

FOR THE CHAAT MIX
10 cherry tomatoes, quartered
2 green chillies, diced
1 red chilli, diced
1 red onion, diced
handful of pomegranate seeds, plus extra to serve
handful of chopped coriander (cilantro), plus extra to serve
handful of chopped mint leaves
zest and juice of 1 lime
pinch of ground cumin
pinch of chaat masala
pinch of salt

FOR THE TOPPINGS
4–5 tablespoons Green Goddess Chutney (page 156)
4–5 tablespoons Apple Raita (page 166)
handful of Bombay mix

Boil the sweet potatoes in a large saucepan filled with salted boiling water for 20–30 minutes until tender. Drain and set aside to cool.

Meanwhile, combine the ingredients for the chaat mix in a large bowl and set aside.

Once the sweet potatoes have cooled, peel off the skins and cut the flesh into cubes.

Heat the olive oil in a large frying pan over a medium heat. Add the cumin seeds and fennel seeds. Once they start crackling and fizzing, add your sweet potato cubes, along with the tarragon, paprika, chaat masala and salt. Toss the sweet potato cubes around the pan to coat in the spices and cook for 2–3 minutes until the sides become crispy, being careful not to break up the sweet potatoes.

Transfer to a serving dish, then spoon the chaat mix all over the top. Dollop and drizzle over the chutney and raita, then sprinkle over the Bombay mix. Garnish with pomegranate seeds and coriander, and serve.

BOMBAY CHEESE TOAST

My first attempt at a complete amalgamation of cultures was making this Bombay Cheese Toast. Papa had a Sunday ritual where he would make cheese on toast packed with beef tomatoes and rings of red onions, using a medium white Cheddar on top of thick slices of freshly baked white bread. It was delicious. I remember watching him spread the bread with salty butter and slicing strips of Cheddar. We'd all sit patiently by the grill, waiting for the onions and tomatoes to blister, and for the cheese to bubble and go golden. The smell was so comforting: it smelled like home.

Another fond memory was going to our cousin's house in Mumbai and eating the famous sandwich of green chutney and masala potatoes on airy white bread. The bread in India is not as dense as the bread we have here; it is lighter in texture, it crisps up and toasts a lot quicker, and it absorbs chutney like a sponge. I took these snippets of nostalgia from both of my homes and made this Bombay Cheese Toast. I have added masala mashed potatoes, green chutney, and a chilli-cheese mix made with brown butter, green chillies, peppers, onions and sharp English Cheddar (I use extra-mature rather than the medium one preferred by my dad), all melted on top of sourdough. Apologies in advance for all glorious smells that will make your stomach rumble as you cook.

4 slices of sourdough bread
2 tablespoons melted ghee
4 tablespoons Green Goddess Chutney (page 156), plus extra to serve
handful of grated mozzarella
handful of grated extra-mature Cheddar
½ red onion, diced
1–2 green chillies, diced
Nanima's Tomato Chutney (page 160), to serve (optional)

FOR THE MASALA MASHED POTATO

1 large potato, peeled and chopped into large chunks
small handful of coriander (cilantro), chopped
pinch of ground turmeric
pinch of ground cumin
½ tablespoon olive oil
sea salt and freshly ground black pepper

Begin by making the masala mashed potato. Boil the potato in a large saucepan of salted boiling water for 12–15 minutes until tender, then drain and transfer to a mixing bowl. Mash with a fork, then add the remaining masala mashed potato ingredients. Season with a pinch of salt and pepper and set aside.

Line a baking tray with baking parchment or foil and preheat the grill to medium.

Lightly toast the sourdough in the toaster until it has a nice crunch. Place the slices on the prepared tray and spread or spoon over most of the melted ghee. Add 1 tablespoon of the Green Goddess Chutney to each slice and spread it all over the toast. Divide the masala mash between the slices, spreading it out into an even layer. Top with the cheeses and sprinkle over the onion and chillies. Finish with a little extra ghee to help it brown and bubble.

Place under the grill for 4–6 minutes until the cheese has bubbled and melted. Serve with a little extra Green Goddess Chutney, a spoonful of Nanima's Tomato Chutney, or as it is with a glass of masala chai!

CAULIFLOWER CHEESE TOAST

SERVES 4

This is one for the cauli-cheese lovers: softly spiced cauliflower, gooey cheese and sweet, tangy mango chutney. This toast is perfect for brunch, lunch, weeknight dinners and any time you need a dose of comfort.

handful of grated mozzarella

handful of grated extra-mature Cheddar

4 slices of crusty sourdough bread

2 tablespoons melted ghee

4 tablespoons mango chutney (shop-bought)

1 spring onion (scallion), sliced

1 large red chilli, finely chopped (optional)

Green Goddess Chutney (page 156), to serve

FOR THE MASALA CAULIFLOWER

1 cauliflower, broken into florets

3–4 tablespoons olive oil or melted butter

1 teaspoon ground coriander

1 teaspoon ground turmeric

1 teaspoon chilli powder

1½ teaspoons garam masala

2–6 green chillies (to taste), chopped

sea salt and freshly ground black pepper

Begin by making the masala cauliflower. Place the cauliflower florets in a steamer basket and steam for 5–10 minutes until fully cooked through.

Transfer to a bowl and add the olive oil or butter. Mash with a fork, then add the remaining masala cauliflower ingredients. Stir in half the mozzarella and half the Cheddar, and season to taste with salt and pepper.

Line a baking tray with baking parchment or foil and preheat the grill to medium.

Lightly toast the sourdough in the toaster until it has a nice crunch. Place the slices on the prepared tray and spread or spoon over most of the melted ghee. Add 1 tablespoon of the mango chutney to each slice and spread it all over the toast. Divide the masala cauliflower between the slices, spreading it out into an even layer. Top with the remaining cheeses and sprinkle over the spring onion and chilli. Finish with a little extra ghee to help it brown and bubble.

Place under the grill for 4–6 minutes until the cheese has bubbled and melted. Serve with a glass of masala chai and some Green Goddess Chutney.

CHILLI PANEER

In this popular Indo-Chinese dish, cubed paneer is cooked in a sweet, sticky, spicy, salty, tangy masala. It's delicious paired with hakka noodles or naans.

FOR THE PANEER
6 tablespoons rice flour
6 tablespoons cornflour (cornstarch)
1 teaspoon salt
1 teaspoon coarsely ground black pepper
600g (1lb 5oz) paneer, cut into bite-sized cubes
vegetable, sunflower or rapeseed oil, for shallow-frying

FOR THE MASALA
1–2 tablespoons olive oil
½ onion, chopped into bite-sized chunks
4 green bird's-eye chillies, halved lengthways
1 tablespoon ginger purée
1 tablespoon garlic purée
½ teaspoon ground turmeric
1 teaspoon ground coriander
2 tablespoons tomato ketchup
1 tablespoon soy sauce
1 teaspoon rice wine vinegar
1½ teaspoons soft light brown sugar
1 large red bell pepper (capsicum), chopped into bite-sized chunks
1 large green bell pepper (capsicum), chopped into bite-sized chunks

TO SERVE
sliced spring onions (scallions)
sliced red chillies

Combine both flours with the salt and pepper in a mixing bowl. Slowly add a splash of water, a little at a time, and stir to make a slurry. Remove 2 tablespoons of the slurry and set aside for the masala. Add the cubed paneer to the bowl with the rest of the slurry and mix well to ensure it is completely coated.

Pour the oil into a heavy-based frying pan to a depth of 1cm (½in) and place over a medium–high heat. Once the oil is hot, check its temperature by dropping in a tiny piece of paneer. It should float and sizzle. If so, the oil is ready to go.

Shallow-fry the paneer, working in small batches so as not to overcrowd the pan. Cook for 3–4 minutes on each side until completely golden and crispy. Set aside on a plate lined with paper towels to drain while you fry the rest.

To make the masala, heat the oil in a wok over a high heat. Add the onion and chillies and sauté for 1–2 minutes until they start to break down and sizzle, then add the ginger, garlic and spices, and cook for 30 seconds. Next add the ketchup, soy sauce, vinegar, sugar and a pinch of salt, and mix well. Sauté for about 30 seconds, then add the red and green peppers and cook for 2 minutes more.

Once the peppers have softened a little, add the fried paneer and reserved slurry, and keep tossing the wok to keep everything moving until the paneer is completely coated and the sauce is clinging to the vegetables and paneer. Taste and adjust the seasoning if needed.

Serve, garnished with sliced spring onions and chillies.

STREET EATS

PRAWN TIKKA TACOS

SERVES 4

After having the privilege of travelling to Mexico, I discovered so many similarities in culture, food and flavour profiles between Mexican food and Indian food. You'll need a good frying pan in order to get a good sear on the prawns. This dish is packed with freshness, crunch, and delicious Indian and Mexican spices.

350g (12oz) raw king (jumbo) prawns, deveined, cleaned and patted dry
2½ tablespoons olive oil
12 small soft corn tortillas
1–2 avocados, peeled, stoned and smashed
6 tablespoons mango chutney (shop-bought)
6 tablespoons soured cream
1 carrot, peeled and grated
2–3 spring onions (scallions), sliced
1–2 large red chillies, diced
handful of coriander (cilantro), chopped
1 lime, sliced into wedges, to serve

FOR THE MARINADE
1 tablespoon garlic purée
small pinch of kasoori methi (dried fenugreek leaves)
1 teaspoon ground turmeric
1 teaspoon chilli flakes
2 tablespoons Greek-style yoghurt
1 teaspoon garam masala
½ teaspoon red chilli paste
pinch of salt

Combine the marinade ingredients in a mixing bowl. Add the prawns and stir to coat, then leave to marinate for at least 15–20 minutes in the refrigerator.

When you're ready to cook, heat 2 tablespoons of the oil in a large frying pan over a medium heat. Once the oil is nice and hot, add the marinated prawns and cook for 1–2 minutes on each side – no longer, as you want them to be cooked through but pink, not overcooked and rubbery. Set aside.

Heat the remaining ½ tablespoon oil in a clean frying pan over a medium heat. Add the tortillas, one at a time, cooking for about 30 seconds per side, then setting aside on a plate to keep warm while you heat up the rest.

To assemble, lay a tortilla on a plate and add some smashed avocado, followed by some mango chutney and soured cream. Add 2–3 prawns, then top with a little grated carrot and some spring onion. Garnish with chillies and coriander. Repeat with the remaining tortillas and fillings, and serve with lime wedges, for squeezing.

SERVES 4

CHIPOTLE CHICKEN TIKKA TACOS

These tacos are a firm favourite: smoky, spicy, juicy chicken; cooling cucumber and soured cream; spicy onions; zingy lime. The flavour is a cross between tandoori chicken and smoked chicken.

2 tablespoons olive oil
12 small soft corn tortillas
¼ red onion, finely sliced
6 tablespoons soured cream
½ cucumber, grated and excess water drained
handful of mint leaves, chopped
6 tablespoons Green Goddess Chutney (page 156)
1 lime, sliced into wedges, to serve

FOR THE CHICKEN TIKKA
600g (1lb 5oz) skinless, boneless chicken thighs
2 tablespoons olive oil
1½ tablespoons garlic purée
1 tablespoon chipotle paste
1 tablespoon tomato paste (concentrated purée)
1 teaspoon ground turmeric
1 teaspoon chilli flakes
zest and juice of 1 large orange
juice of 1 lime
1 teaspoon coarsely ground black pepper
1 teaspoon ground cumin
½ teaspoon red chilli paste
pinch of salt
2 tablespoons runny honey

In a mixing bowl, combine all the chicken tikka ingredients except for the honey and mix well to coat. Allow the chicken to marinate for at least 15–20 minutes in the refrigerator.

Preheat your oven to 175°C (330°F/gas mark 3–4) and line a baking tray with foil.

Transfer the marinated chicken into the prepared baking tray and roast for 25–30 minutes until cooked through. Remove from the oven and drizzle the honey over the top. Using a fork and sharp knife, shred the chicken inside the tray, allowing all the juices to soak into the chicken. Set aside.

Heat the oil in a clean frying pan over a medium heat. Add the tortillas, one at a time, cooking for about 30 seconds per side, then setting aside on a plate to keep warm while you heat up the rest.

To assemble, lay a tortilla on a plate and add some red onion slices, followed by 1–2 spoonfuls of shredded chicken. Top with 1 teaspoon of the soured cream, then a little grated cucumber and some chopped mint. Garnish with zig-zags of the Green Goddess Chutney. Repeat with the remaining tortillas and fillings, and serve with lime wedges, for squeezing.

OVERLEAF *Prawn Tikka Tacos and Chipotle Chicken Tikka Tacos*

HARISSA CHAPALI LAMB KEBAB

SERVES 4–6

This type of kebab originated in Pakistan. 'Chapali' means flat and is derived from the Pashto word chapleet. I have added harissa paste for smokiness and herbal notes, and dried apricots for juiciness and sweetness. Here, I've given instructions for how to make these kebabs in a frying pan with a little oil, but you can also bake them in the oven, or even stick them under the grill or on the barbecue. I love to serve these kebabs with my Apple Raita (page 166) or Pomegranate Raita (page 162); the sweetness and spiciness works well the smoky, harissa-spiced meat.

8 dried apricots
1kg (2lb 4oz) lamb mince (20 per cent fat)
1 red onion, diced
1½ teaspoons salt
1 tablespoon coarsely ground black pepper
2 tablespoons garlic purée
1 tablespoon ginger purée
1 egg
4 tablespoons dried breadcrumbs
2 tablespoons tomato paste (concentrated purée)
1 teaspoon garam masala
1 tablespoon harissa paste
1–2 chopped green chillies
1 tablespoon olive oil or rapeseed oil

Soak the apricots in a bowl of lukewarm water for 3 hours or overnight to rehydrate. Drain, squeeze out the excess water, and chop into small pieces. Add to a large mixing bowl, and add all the other ingredients except the oil. Mix very well.

Using your hands (see tip), divide the mixture into six and form each portion into a round patty, pressing them down a little bit so they are flatter.

Heat the oil in a large frying pan over a medium–high heat. Once the oil is hot, reduce the heat to medium and add the kebabs to the pan, working in batches of about 3 at a time depending on the size of your pan. Cook on each side for 6–8 minutes until cooked through, then keep warm while you cook the rest. Serve with your favourite raita.

TIP *Grease your hands with a little oil to stop the mince from sticking to your fingers. This will make the patties much easier to shape.*

SERVES 3–4

HOT HONEY GARLIC PRAWNS

I love these prawns; they are delicious served on top of some sourdough spread with melted salty butter, or with my Hakka Noodles on page 31. You could even serve them inside a brioche hot dog roll with a dollop of my Caramelised Garlic Raita (page 167) and some baby gem lettuce.

- 400g (14oz) raw king (jumbo) prawns, heads and tails removed, deveined and butterflied
- 2 tablespoons ghee
- ⅓ teaspoon mustard seeds
- ⅓ teaspoon ajwain seeds
- 1 tablespoon tomato paste (concentrated purée)
- 1 tablespoon garlic purée
- 1 teaspoon ginger purée
- 2–3 green bird's-eye chillies, diced
- 1 tablespoon rice vinegar
- 1 tablespoon light soy sauce
- handful of coriander (cilantro), chopped
- 2 spring onions (scallions), chopped
- juice of ½ lime
- 1½ tablespoons runny honey

FOR THE MARINADE
- ½ tablespoon rice vinegar
- 1 tablespoon light soy sauce
- pinch of salt

Combine the marinade ingredients in a shallow bowl. Add the prawns and marinate for 10 minutes.

Heat the ghee in a deep skillet over a medium heat. Once the ghee releases its aromas, add the mustard seeds and ajwain seeds, and allow the spices to crackle for about 10 seconds. Reduce the heat to medium–low and add the tomato paste, garlic and ginger purée and chillies. Sauté for 1–2 minutes until the mixture smells and the ghee starts to rise to the top through the masala base.

Add the vinegar and soy sauce and sauté for another minute, then add the marinated prawns and cook for 2–3 minutes on each side until they turn pink.

Transfer the prawns and sauce to a mixing bowl. Add the coriander, spring onions, lime juice and honey and mix well.

Serve with your desired accompaniments and enjoy!

STREET EATS

BURRATA WITH CUMIN-ROASTED VEGETABLES

SERVES 4

One of the best things in life is a creamy, wobbly and bursting burrata. Here, it is paired with cumin-spiced vegetables, and served with fresh herbs and a sweet, spicy, juicy dressing. Absolutely heavenly.

1 courgette (zucchini), sliced into chunks
1 large aubergine (eggplant), sliced into chunks
1 red Romano pepper, sliced into chunks
1 red onion, sliced into wedges
1–2 red chillies, sliced
1 tablespoon cumin seeds
2 tablespoons garlic purée
4 tablespoons olive oil
65g (1¾oz) peas (thawed if using frozen)
100g (3½oz) baby-leaf spinach
100g (3½oz) parsley leaves, roughly chopped (discard the stalks), plus extra to serve (optional)
handful of freshly chopped mint, plus extra to serve (optional)
1 whole burrata (about 150g/5½oz)
salt and freshly ground black pepper

FOR THE DRESSING
2 tablespoons olive oil
1 tablespoon red wine vinegar
1 tablespoon maple syrup
pinch of chilli flakes
zest and juice of 1 orange

Preheat the oven to 170°C (325°F/gas mark 3) and line a baking tray with foil.

In a mixing bowl, combine the courgette, aubergine, pepper, onion, chillies, cumin seeds and garlic. Season with a generous pinch of salt and pepper and drizzle over the oil. Give it all a good mix so the vegetables are well coated in the oils and spices.

Spread out the vegetables on the prepared baking tray and roast for 25–30 minutes until the vegetables have blistered and softened but are still a little al dente. Add the thawed peas to the baking tray and set aside so the veg can cool.

Once the vegetables have cooled to room temperature, tip them into a mixing bowl and add the spinach, parsley and mint.

In a separate bowl, combine all the dressing ingredients and mix very well. Season with salt and pepper, then pour over the fresh herbs and roasted vegetables. Gently mix together, then transfer to a serving dish.

Place the burrata on top, and garnish with extra herbs if you desire.

CAULIFLOWER POPPERS
BANG BANG GOBI

SERVES 4–6

This dish is delicious as a snack. I love to serve it with ice-cold beer or one of my gin tipples! It also makes the perfect side dish to my Hakka Noodles (page 31).

1 large cauliflower, cut into bite-sized florets
100ml (3½fl oz) milk

FOR THE COATING
70g (2½oz) panko breadcrumbs
1 teaspoon freshly ground black pepper
1 teaspoon salt
1 teaspoon ground cumin
1 teaspoon garlic powder
1 teaspoon ground turmeric

FOR THE BANG BANG SAUCE
1 tablespoon sriracha
1 tablespoon mango chutney (shop-bought)
1 tablespoon maple syrup
2 tablespoons mayonnaise
1 teaspoon garam masala
½ teaspoon smoked paprika
salt

TO SERVE
1 small red chilli, finely sliced (optional)
handful of chopped chives
lime wedges

Preheat the oven to 170°C (325°F/gas mark 3) and line a baking tray with baking parchment.

Par-boil the cauliflower in a saucepan of boiling water for 6–7 minutes until slightly softened, then drain and allow to cool slightly.

In a shallow bowl, mix together all the ingredients for the coating. Pour the milk into a separate bowl.

Dip the cauliflower florets into the milk, then roll them in the coating mixture. Place them on the prepared baking tray, making sure they aren't touching.

Bake for 15 minutes until starting to turn crisp and golden brown, then use a flat spatula to carefully turn them, ensuring the coating doesn't come off, and bake for another 15 minutes on the other side.

Meanwhile, to make the bang bang sauce, simply mix all the ingredients together in a bowl and season with salt to taste.

To serve, drizzle the bang bang sauce over the cauliflower and scatter over the red chilli and chives. Serve with lime wedges for squeezing.

TIP *You can make this dish vegan by swapping the mayonnaise for vegan mayonnaise and the milk for any plant-based milk.*

CHINESE CHILLI PRAWNS

SERVES 4–5

This recipe is an ode to my Nani; she absolutely loved Chinese and Indo-Chinese food, and her favourite dish was chilli prawns. You will need a wok or a heavy-based Kahari-style dish for this recipe.

- 2 tablespoons olive oil or sesame oil
- 1 teaspoon fennel seeds
- 2 green bird's-eye chillies, chopped
- 1 tablespoon garlic purée
- 1 tablespoon ginger purée
- 700g (1lb 9oz) raw jumbo king prawns, deveined, butterflied and cleaned
- 1 tablespoon Chinese five-spice
- 1 tablespoon white rice vinegar
- 2 tablespoons tomato ketchup
- 1 tablespoon black bean sauce
- ½ teaspoon garam masala
- 1 tablespoon soft light brown sugar

TO SERVE
- 2 spring onions (scallions), chopped
- 1 red chilli, sliced
- handful of chopped coriander (cilantro)

Heat a wok over a high heat. Once hot, add the oil. Once the oil is hot, reduce the temperature to medium, then add the fennel seeds, bird's-eye chillies, garlic and ginger, and wait for everything to sizzle and for the aromas to be released – this will take 20–30 seconds, but keep the mixture moving in the pan all the while.

Add the prawns and fry for 2–3 minutes until they start to go a little pink, keeping them moving all the time. Add all the remaining ingredients (except the 'to serve' items) and cook for 2–3 minutes so it can all come together. Keep the prawns moving the whole time, and don't overcook them; you just want them to turn pink and the flesh to turn white.

Transfer to your serving dish and garnish with the spring onions, chilli and coriander, then enjoy!

STREET EATS

BUNS & PAOS

This chapter is all about unique buns and 'paos', as they're known in Hindi (white bread rolls). Who doesn't love a good burger, or the comfort of something carby and hearty that you can enjoy in all weathers?

These recipes can be made all year round for brunch, lunch or dinner. Serve them as the main event with chips (fries) or salads, or pair with other dishes from the book for a real feast.

PAO BHAJI

SERVES 4–6

Mumbai's most beloved and classic street food, consisting of a thick, spicy vegetable curry served with pao, a soft bread roll spread with butter.

2 large baking potatoes, peeled and chopped
4 carrots, peeled and chopped
65g (2¼oz) peas (thawed if using frozen)
4 tablespoons ghee
6–8 fresh curry leaves
1 teaspoon cumin seeds
2 onions, diced
1 tablespoon ginger purée
1½ tablespoons garlic purée
1–3 green bird's-eye chillies (depending on how spicy you like it), chopped
3 tablespoons tomato paste (concentrated purée)
1 teaspoon ground turmeric
1 teaspoon ground coriander
handful of coriander (cilantro), chopped, plus extra to serve
salt

TO SERVE
8–12 white dinner rolls (2 per person)
salted butter, for spreading
lemon wedges

Bring a large saucepan of water to the boil. Add the potatoes and carrots and boil them for 15–20 minutes until soft, adding the peas for the last 2 minutes. Drain, then set aside and allow to cool.

Once cooled, tip the boiled veg into a bowl and mash well using a fork. Set aside.

Melt the ghee in a large heavy-based frying pan over a medium heat. Add the curry leaves and cumin seeds and cook for 20 seconds until fragrant, then add the onions. Stir and cook for about 8 minutes until softened and browned. Stir in the ginger, garlic and chillies, and season with a pinch of salt, then add the mashed vegetables, tomato paste, ground spices and coriander, mixing well. Cover and cook for 5–8 minutes.

If you prefer the texture to be a little wetter, then add a splash of water to the pan and season with salt once more.

Cut the dinner rolls in half and spread with the butter. Lightly sear in a dry frying pan over a medium heat for just 10–20 seconds until the bread is lightly browned.

Divide the bhaji between bowls, and serve with the lightly toasted buttered rolls and lemon wedges for squeezing. Scatter over some coriander and enjoy!

TANDOORI CHICKEN BURGER

SERVES 4

The king of all burgers. Here, a juicy chicken tikka that is packed with flavour is dressed in condiments and paired with delicious garnishes. These burgers will soon become a staple in your home. Feel free to change the salad ingredients inside the bun and really make it your own.

FOR THE CHICKEN TIKKA
500g (1lb 2oz) boneless, skinless chicken thighs
2 tablespoons olive oil
1 tablespoon tomato paste (concentrated purée)
2 tablespoons Greek-style yoghurt
1 tablespoon garlic purée
½ tablespoon ginger purée
1 teaspoon salt
1 teaspoon tandoori masala (available in most major supermarkets)
½ teaspoon ground turmeric
1 teaspoon ground cumin
1 teaspoon kasoori methi (dried fenugreek leaves)

FOR THE BUNS
4 tablespoons mango chutney (shop-bought)
4 tablespoons Caramelised Garlic Raita (page 167)
4 brioche burger buns, halved
large handful of shredded iceberg lettuce
1 beef tomato, sliced
½ cucumber, sliced into rounds
pinch of chaat masala
4 slices of Gouda cheese

In a large mixing bowl, combine all the ingredients for the chicken tikka, making sure the chicken is well coated. Leave to marinate for at least 15–20 minutes in the refrigerator (overnight is better, if you have time).

Preheat the oven to 190°C (375°F/gas mark 5) and line a baking tray with baking parchment or foil.

Spread out the marinated chicken on the prepared tray and roast for 25–30 minutes until well cooked, turning halfway through.

To build your burgers, spread the chutney and raita on both sides of the buns, then layer lettuce, tomato and cucumber slices on the base of each bun. Top with the chicken pieces, then sprinkle with chaat masala. Add a slice of Gouda and close the buns!

SERVES 4

PANEER TIKKA BURGER

This is the ultimate vegetarian burger: juicy marinated paneer tikka, spicy sauces, fresh garnishes and aioli, all served in a buttery brioche bun.

500g (5½oz) block of paneer, sliced lengthways into 4 slices, each about 1cm (½in) thick (you may have enough to make 6 burgers)
4 brioche burger buns, halved
aioli or mayonnaise
ketchup, sriracha or Grilled Pineapple Chutney (page 157)
large handful of shredded iceberg lettuce
1 beef tomato, sliced
½ cucumber, cut into rounds
chaat masala, for sprinkling

FOR THE TIKKA MARINADE
2 tablespoons olive oil
2 tablespoons Greek-style yoghurt
1 tablespoon garlic purée
½ tablespoon ginger purée
1 teaspoon salt
1 teaspoon ground turmeric
1 teaspoon ground cumin

Combine all the ingredients for the marinade in a mixing bowl. Add the paneer and turn to coat in the marinade. Leave to marinate for 10 minutes.

When you're ready to cook, preheat the oven to 180°C (350°F/gas mark 4) and line a baking tray with baking parchment or foil.

Place the paneer slices in the prepared tray and cook for 15–20 minutes, flipping them halfway through. Ensure the paneer is well cooked; it should be slightly crispy on the outside and springy to the touch.

To build your burgers, spread the brioche buns with your chosen condiments, then pile up the lettuce, tomato and cucumber slices on the base of each bun. Top with the paneer slices, sprinkle over the chaat masala and close the buns. Enjoy with a lovely cold drink.

SERVES 1

PAPA'S OMELETTE BUN

As kids, we would often collect fresh eggs from our neighbours that would still be warm as they had just been laid, and we would use them to make delicious omelettes, egg bhurji and shakshuka. Papa used to make this bun as his go-to meal for us when we were growing up – and what an absolute treat it was. Fresh eggs and a cheesy masala omelette, packed with flavour and delicious served in a brioche burger bun!

2 large eggs, beaten
handful of grated mature Cheddar
1 green chilli, chopped
¼ red onion, chopped
5 cherry tomatoes, chopped
pinch of chilli powder
pinch of ground cumin
pinch of ground turmeric
small handful of coriander (cilantro)
knob of butter or ghee, for cooking
salt

TO SERVE
brioche burger bun or sourdough bread slices
butter, for spreading
condiment(s) of your choice

In a large mixing bowl, combine all the ingredients except the butter or ghee and 'to serve' items. Mix well and season with a pinch of salt.

Melt the butter or ghee in a good-quality frying pan over a medium heat. Once it has melted completely, pour in the egg mixture and cook for 3–6 minutes until the bottom goes golden and crispy. Once golden, either flip the omelette over like a pancake to cook on the other side for 3–6 minutes, or use a spatula to gently fold and flip it so the other side cooks.

Meanwhile, lightly toast your bun or sourdough slices and spread with a little butter, along with the condiment(s) of your choice.

Once the omelette is ready, fold it in half if needed and place inside the bun. Happy, happy days!

BUNS & PAOS

POTATO DUMPLING PAO
VADA PAO

SERVES 6

Mumbai's famous street burger, made up of a white dinner roll, vada, which is a spiced and fried potato dumpling, and chutneys of your choice – I would recommend Mama's Peanut Chutney (page 158), Green Goddess Chutney (page 156) and a shop-bought mango or tamarind chutney for this recipe. This dish is best enjoyed with a glass of fresh masala chai – oh, how very Bombay!

- 3 large baking potatoes, peeled and chopped into chunks
- 1 tablespoon garlic purée
- 1 tablespoon ginger purée
- 1 teaspoon chaat masala
- 3 green bird's-eye chillies, finely chopped
- ½ teaspoon ground turmeric
- ½ teaspoon onion powder
- small handful of coriander (cilantro), chopped
- 1 tablespoon olive oil or mustard oil
- ½ teaspoon cumin seeds
- ½ teaspoon mustard seeds
- 10 fresh curry leaves
- vegetable oil, for frying

FOR THE PAKORA BATTER
- 230g (8oz) gram flour (also known as chickpea or besan flour)
- ½ teaspoon ground turmeric
- pinch of bicarbonate of soda (baking soda) (optional)
- 100ml (3½fl oz) room-temperature water
- pinch of salt
- 1 teaspoon chilli powder

TO SERVE
- 6 white dinner rolls (1 per person)
- Mama's Peanut Chutney (page 158)
- Green Goddess Chutney (page 156)
- mango or tamarind chutney (shop-bought)
- fried green chillies (optional; see below)

Bring a large saucepan of water to the boil. Add the potatoes and boil for 15–20 minutes until soft. Drain, then set aside and allow to cool.

Tip the cooled potatoes into a mixing bowl and mash with a fork. Add the garlic and ginger purées, along with the chaat masala, chillies, turmeric, onion powder and coriander. Mix well to combine.

Heat the olive oil or mustard oil in a frying pan over a medium heat. Once hot, add the cumin seeds, mustard seeds and curry leaves and sizzle for 10–20 seconds until fragrant. Allow to cool to room temperature, then add to the potato mix and combine well.

Using your hands, form the mixture into 6 palm-sized patties. Place on a tray lined with baking parchment and put in the freezer for 30 minutes to firm up.

Meanwhile, in a different mixing bowl, combine all the ingredients for the batter and whisk to combine.

Pour the vegetable oil into a large wok or karahi to a depth of 3cm (1¼in) and heat over a medium heat. Test the oil to see if it's hot enough by dropping a little of the batter into it; if it sizzles and floats to the top immediately, the oil is ready for frying the *vadas*.

Take the *vada* patties out of the freezer. Working in batches so as not to overcrowd the pan, dip each one into the batter to coat it evenly, then carefully drop into the hot oil. Fry for 3 minutes on each side until golden brown and crispy. Keep them moving around in the hot oil as they cook. Set aside the fried *vadas* on a plate lined with paper towels to absorb excess oil while you cook the rest.

To assemble, slice the bread rolls without breaking them in half and spread with the chutneys. Tuck the *vadas* inside, garnish with the chillies and enjoy.

FRIED GREEN CHILLIES *To make the fried green chilli garnish, heat 1 tablespoon olive oil in a small frying pan over a medium heat. Once the oil is hot, add 4–6 whole green chillies, including the stalks. Stand back and allow the skins of the chillies to fry and blister. This will only take 10–20 seconds. Carefully remove them from the oil and set aside to serve as a garnish.*

SERVES 4–6

LAMB & EGGS
KEEMA PAR EDA

A deliciously moreish Parsi dish that is a staple in Mumbai and a favourite in Delhi. Of course, it has been given a little more depth here in this recipe. Deliciously spiced lamb mince is paired with fried eggs, chilli and feta.

2 tablespoons olive oil
1 teaspoon fennel seeds
1 teaspoon cumin seeds
1 onion, roughly chopped
3–4 green bird's-eye chillies, chopped
2 tablespoons garlic purée
1 tablespoon ginger purée
550g (1lb 4oz) lean lamb mince
2 tomatoes, chopped
½ teaspoon ground turmeric
2 bay leaves
1 cinnamon stick
1 teaspoon chilli powder, plus extra to season
1 teaspoon ground coriander
1 tablespoon soft dark brown sugar
2 tablespoons fresh lemon juice
1–2 teaspoons salt (to taste)
6 eggs
salt and freshly ground black pepper

TO SERVE
white dinner rolls or focaccia slices
butter, for spreading
handful of coriander (cilantro), chopped
handful of crumbled feta (optional)
Chilli Garlic Pesto (page 161)

Heat the oil in a heavy-based frying pan over a medium heat. Once the oil is hot, add the fennel and cumin seeds and allow to pop and sizzle for 10 seconds, then add the onion, chillies, garlic and ginger. Cover and cook for 8–10 minutes until softened and browned.

Stir in the remaining ingredients except the eggs and 'to serve' items. Season well, then cover once more and cook for a further 10 minutes until the mince has broken down and released its water and fat, stirring intermittently so the mixture does not catch at the bottom.

Check your mince and season to taste once more, then leave the lid off for a few minutes to let the juices evaporate a little. When you're ready, use a spoon to make 6 small wells in the mince, each big enough to hold an egg. Carefully crack the eggs into these little wells, taking care not to break the yolks. Season each egg with a little salt and chilli powder.

Cover with the lid once more and cook for a further 4–8 minutes, checking often, until the eggs are cooked but the yolk is runny.

Meanwhile, toast your white rolls or focaccia and spread with butter.

When everything is ready, garnish the delicious keema mixture with coriander and feta, and serve with the buttered toasted white rolls or focaccia and the pesto.

BUNS & PAOS

POTATO CHICKPEA BURGER
BUN TIKKI

SERVES 4

This is my take on an Indian vegetarian sloppy joe and aloo burger. It is made with chutneys, a potato smash and a spicy chickpea curry, with a little Bombay mix for added crunch.

FOR THE ALOO SMASH
2 large baking potatoes, peeled and chopped into chunks
65g (1¾oz) peas (thawed if using frozen)
½ teaspoon ground turmeric
1–2 red bird's-eye chillies, chopped
½ teaspoon chaat masala
½ teaspoon onion powder
½ red onion, chopped
handful of coriander (cilantro), chopped
1 teaspoon salt

FOR THE CHICKPEA MASALA
1 tablespoon ghee
1 teaspoon cumin seeds
1 onion, diced
1 teaspoon chilli powder
1 teaspoon garlic purée
1 teaspoon ginger purée
350g (12oz) canned chickpeas, rinsed and drained
1 tablespoon tomato paste (concentrated purée)
1 tablespoon garam masala
1 teaspoon ground turmeric
125ml (4fl oz/½ cup) boiling water
salt

FOR THE BUNS
4 burger buns, halved
ghee, for spreading
Apple Raita (page 166)
tamarind chutney (shop-bought)
large handful of Bombay mix
large handful of coriander (cilantro), chopped
½ red onion, chopped

Begin by making the aloo smash. Bring a large saucepan of water to the boil. Add the potatoes and boil for 15–20 minutes until soft, adding the peas for the final 2 minutes. Drain, then set aside and allow to cool.

Once cooled, tip the potatoes and peas into a mixing bowl. Add the remaining aloo smash ingredients and mash it all together with your hands until well combined. Season to taste and set aside to keep warm.

To make the chickpea masala, melt the ghee in a heavy-based saucepan over a medium heat. Once hot, add the cumin seeds and allow to pop and sizzle for about 10 seconds, then add the onion, chilli powder, garlic and ginger. Cover and cook for 8–10 minutes until softened and browned.

Add the remaining chickpea masala ingredients, plus a generous pinch of salt, and cook for a further 10 minutes. The texture of the curry should be thick and free-flowing.

To assemble, toast the burger buns in a dry frying pan until just golden, then spread each half of each bun with a little ghee, followed by the raita and chutneys. Place 1½ tablespoons of the aloo smash on the bottom half of each bun and roughly spread it out, then spoon over 2 tablespoons of the chickpea masala curry (or more to taste) for each bun. Sprinkle the Bombay mix over the top, then scatter with the fresh coriander and red onion. Close the buns and enjoy.

MASALA SHAKSHUKA

SERVES 4-6

This is my family's favourite brunch, but it also makes a great quick supper dish. You can really make this shakshuka your own by topping it with different proteins, vegetables, pickles, avocado – anything you like, really. It has its origins in Libya, Morocco and Tunisia, and is a hearty dish of stewed vegetables, tomatoes and eggs. My recipe incorporates Indian spices, along with meatiness from the mushrooms and sweetness from the peppers, all of which pair perfectly with the drippy egg yolks.

2 tablespoons ghee or olive oil
1 teaspoon ajwain seeds
1 large onion, chopped
2 tablespoons tomato paste (concentrated purée)
1 tablespoon ginger purée
1 tablespoon garlic purée
2–3 green bird's-eye chillies, chopped
1 teaspoon ground cumin
1 teaspoon ground coriander
½ teaspoon ground turmeric
2 portobello mushrooms, chopped into chunks
1 red bell pepper (capsicum), chopped into chunks
1 green bell pepper (capsicum), chopped into chunks
2 tablespoons cream cheese (optional)
6–8 medium eggs
salt and freshly ground black pepper

TO SERVE
handful of chopped coriander (cilantro)
1 red chilli, sliced
pickled red cabbage (shop-bought)
Chilli Garlic Pesto (page 161) (optional)

Heat the oil in a heavy-based frying pan over a medium heat. Once hot, add the ajwain seeds and let them pop and fizz for 10 seconds, then add the onion, tomato paste, ginger, garlic and bird's-eye chillies, along with the ground spices. Cook this masala base for 5–8 minutes until the onions are soft.

Add the mushrooms and peppers and cook for another 5–8 minutes until softened, then season with a generous pinch of salt. Add a splash of water to loosen and stir through the cream cheese (if using).

Make 6–8 small wells in the masala using your spoon, and crack an egg into each well. Season the eggs with salt and pepper, then cover the pan with a lid and allow the eggs to cook for 3–4 minutes, making sure the yolks are still runny.

Garnish with the coriander, red chilli and pickled red cabbage, then dollop over the pesto, if using. I like to serve this with warm buttery toasted rolls or English muffins.

EGG BHURJI PAO

SERVES 4

This egg bhurji is delicious served as a pao in a toasted buttered brioche roll or toasted dinner roll as I have suggested here. It's also great with my Plain Naan (see page 144).

6–8 eggs
2 tomatoes, chopped
2–3 green bird's-eye chillies, chopped
2 tablespoons chopped coriander (cilantro)
½ teaspoon ground turmeric
2 tablespoons soured cream (optional – if you love creamy scrambled eggs, this is a game-changer)
1½ tablespoons ghee
½ teaspoon cumin seeds
2–3 spring onions (scallions), chopped
salt and freshly ground black pepper

TO SERVE
8 white dinner rolls
butter, for spreading

In a mixing bowl, lightly beat the eggs. Add all the remaining ingredients except the 'to serve' items and the ghee, cumin seeds and spring onions. Mix well, season with salt and a good crack of black pepper, and set aside.

Melt the ghee in a non-stick frying pan over a medium heat. Once hot, add the cumin seeds and let them pop and sizzle for 10 seconds, then add the spring onions and let them soften and go a little brown for about 2 minutes. Now pour in the beaten egg mixture and cook for 3–5 minutes, stirring, until it scrambles to your desired texture.

Meanwhile, lightly toast the rolls and spread with a little butter.

Season the bhurji to taste, pile it into the buns and enjoy.

SERVES 4

CHICKEN KEBAB BURGER

The beauty of this burger is that any condiment works, from chutneys and raitas to ketchup, mayo and barbecue sauce – even burger sauce!

700g (1lb 9oz) chicken mince
1 medium egg
1 tablespoon garlic purée
1 tablespoon ginger purée
1 tablespoon tomato paste (concentrated purée)
1–3 green chillies, diced
1 red onion, diced
handful of finely chopped coriander (cilantro)
1 teaspoon ground cumin
1 teaspoon ground coriander
1 teaspoon ground turmeric
1 teaspoon smoky paprika
1 tablespoon fennel seeds
olive oil, for drizzling
salt and freshly ground black pepper

TO SERVE
4 brioche burger buns, halved
condiments of your choice (see intro)
2 large handfuls of shredded iceberg lettuce
chaat masala, for sprinkling
4 slices of beef tomato
4 tablespoons cream cheese
4 tablespoons pickled cabbage

Preheat the oven to 180°C (350°F/gas mark 4) and line a baking tray with foil.

In a large bowl, combine all the chicken burger ingredients except the olive oil and mix well. Season generously with salt and pepper, and shape into 4 burgers using clean hands. Place the burgers on the prepared tray, drizzle with a little olive oil, and cook in the oven for 25–30 minutes, flipping them halfway through, until cooked through.

To build your burgers, spread both halves of each brioche bun with your chosen condiment, then add some lettuce to the base of each bun. Top with the chicken burgers and sprinkle with chaat masala, then add the tomato slices, cream cheese and pickled cabbage on top. Close the buns and enjoy.

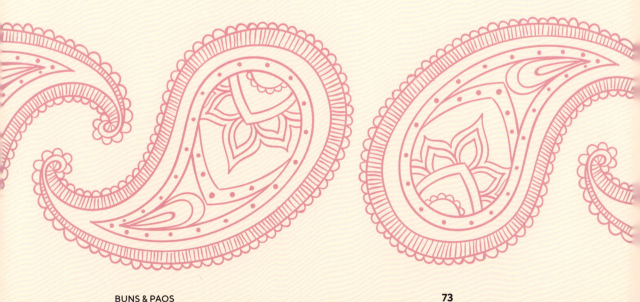

BUNS & PAOS

LAMB KEBAB BURGER

This is one of my favourite burgers. With juicy, flavour-packed lamb, sweet, caramelised onions, punchy, creamy goat's cheese, the freshness of the lettuce and cucumbers and the hum of garlic aioli, it's everything you could want in a burger.

500g (1lb 2oz) lamb mince
1 medium egg
1 tablespoon garlic purée
1 tablespoon ginger purée
1 tablespoon tomato paste (concentrated purée)
1–3 green bird's-eye chillies, diced
1 red onion, diced
handful of mint leaves, finely chopped
1 teaspoon ground cumin
1 teaspoon garam masala
1 teaspoon dried rosemary
olive oil, for drizzling
salt and freshly ground black pepper

TO SERVE
4 brioche burger buns, halved
aioli, for spreading
2 large handfuls of shredded iceberg lettuce
chaat masala, for sprinkling
4 tablespoons caramelised onions
4 slices of soft goat's cheese (or any cheese of your choice)
½ cucumber, sliced

Preheat the oven to 200°C (400°F/gas mark 6) and line a baking tray with foil.

In a large bowl, combine all the lamb burger ingredients except the olive oil and mix well. Season generously with salt and pepper, and shape into 4 burgers using clean hands. Place the burgers on the prepared tray, drizzle with a little olive oil, and cook in the oven for 25–30 minutes, flipping them halfway through, until cooked through.

To build your burgers, spread both halves of each brioche bun with aioli, then add some lettuce to the base of each bun. Top with the lamb burgers and sprinkle with chaat masala, then add the caramelised onions, goat's cheese and cucumber slices on top. Close the buns and enjoy.

TRADITIONAL EATS

This is the chapter that all curry-lovers will seek out and be excited to explore. Here, I will show you how to make some of the most delicious curries you will ever make, all of which are virtually fuss-free. These curries have been designed with your spice box in mind, and are incredibly delicious served with rice or bread – or both!

The secret to a fantastic curry that won't make you feel bloated is to layer the spices and cook them well – don't rush it.

In this chapter, you will taste influences from Punjab, Rajasthan, Mumbai, Delhi, Kerala and Hyderabad.

RAJASTHANI LAMB CURRY

A delicious, spicy, hearty and tender lamb curry originating from Rajasthan in India.

1½ tablespoons ghee
1 tablespoon vegetable oil
3 bay leaves
1–2 cinnamon sticks
2 dried red chillies
1 tablespoon cumin seeds
1½ onions, diced
3 tablespoons garlic purée
2 tablespoons ginger purée
2 green chillies, chopped
500g (1lb 2oz) skinless diced lamb shoulder, trimmed of fat and off the bone
3 tablespoons tomato paste (concentrated purée)
2 tablespoons garam masala
1 tablespoon ground turmeric
1 tablespoon ground coriander
1 teaspoon ground cardamom
375ml (13fl oz/1½ cups) boiling water
sea salt and freshly ground black pepper

TO SERVE
chopped coriander (cilantro)
thumb-sized piece of ginger, chopped into matchsticks

Heat the ghee and vegetable oil in a deep, heavy-based frying pan over a medium heat. Once hot, throw in the bay leaves, cinnamon sticks, dried chillies and cumin seeds, and let it all pop and sizzle for 15–20 seconds until the aromas are released.

Add the onions and fry for 3–4 minutes, letting them caramelise and brown really well, then season with a pinch of salt and add the garlic, ginger and green chillies. Cover and cook for another 3–4 minutes until browned and softened.

Add the lamb and cook for 5 minutes to brown and seal, then add the tomato paste and all the ground spices. Season again with salt and pepper. Let it cook for 5 minutes, then reduce the heat to low and add the boiling water.

Cover and leave to reduce for 1 hour, checking every 20–30 minutes to ensure it is not catching at the bottom. When it's ready, the meat should be tender and the gravy dark and thick. Take off the heat and let it sit for 5 minutes, seasoning once more with salt and pepper if needed.

Garnish with coriander and ginger matchsticks and serve.

CHICKEN OR PANEER MAKHANI

SERVES 4-6

This is the recipe that put Bindas on the map. It is our best-selling and most sought-after curry: butter chicken. A truly decadent, creamy, herby, slightly spicy, slightly sweet curry made with cream and tomatoes. I am sure there will be a permanent fold or bookmark kept on this page. You can use chicken or paneer for this recipe.

700g (1lb 7oz) boneless, skinless chicken thighs, cut into bite-sized pieces, or 600g (1lb 5oz) paneer, cut into cubes
handful of coriander (cilantro), chopped, to serve (optional)

FOR THE MARINADE
2 tablespoons Greek-style yoghurt
2 tablespoons ghee, melted
1 tablespoon garlic purée
1 tablespoon ginger purée
1 teaspoon tomato paste (concentrated purée)
1½ teaspoons ground cumin
1 teaspoon ground turmeric
1 teaspoon garam masala
1 tablespoon chilli powder
1 teaspoon salt

FOR THE MAKHANI SAUCE
3–4 tablespoons ghee
1 onion, finely chopped
2 green bird's-eye chillies, finely chopped
2 tablespoons garlic purée
2 tablespoons ginger purée
1½ teaspoons ground cumin
1 teaspoon ground coriander
1½ teaspoons ground turmeric
1 teaspoon chilli powder
1 teaspoon ground green cardamom
1½ teaspoons garam masala
1–2 teaspoons salt, according to taste
200g (7oz) canned plum tomatoes, puréed
1½ teaspoons caster (superfine) sugar
300ml (10½fl oz) double (heavy) cream, plus extra to serve
3 teaspoons kasoori methi (dried fenugreek leaves)

Combine all the marinade ingredients in a large bowl. Add the chicken or paneer to the marinade and stir to coat. Leave to marinate in the refrigerator for at least 2 hours, preferably overnight.

Preheat the oven to 175°C (330°F/gas mark 3–5). Line a baking tray with foil.

Transfer the marinated chicken or paneer to the prepared tray and roast for 25–30 minutes until tender – do not overcook.

Meanwhile, prepare the makhani sauce. Heat the ghee in a large, heavy-based saucepan over a medium–high heat. Add the onion, chillies, and garlic and ginger purées, and cook for 5–7 minutes, stirring occasionally, until the onion is brown and caramelised.

Add the ground spices and salt, along with the puréed tomatoes, and reduce the heat to medium–low. Cover and cook for 10 minutes, then stir in the sugar and reduce the heat to low. Allow the sauce to gently bubble for 2 minutes, then take the pan off the heat.

Use a hand blender to purée the sauce until nice and smooth, then return it to a medium heat. Cover and cook for 5 minutes, stirring every minute or so. Once the ghee starts rising to the surface, add in the cream, then crush the kasoori methi in your hands and sprinkle those in too.

Once the chicken or paneer is ready, add it to the sauce, along with 6–7 tablespoons of the juices from the tray. Cook over a low heat for 2 minutes to combine, then transfer to a serving dish. Swirl in another tablespoon of cream, sprinkle over the coriander and enjoy.

DAAL MAKHANI

SERVES 4–6

One of the most popular vegetarian Indian dishes, this is a labour of love as you will need to soak the legumes the night before to aid the cooking process. If you do this, you will have the most wonderful, velvety, buttery, creamy daal makhani. I am from North India, and this daal is a staple there, enjoyed on special occasions with loved ones.

200g (7oz) urad dal/black lentils
50g (1¾oz) dried kidney beans

FOR THE MASALA

2½ tablespoons ghee, plus extra to serve
1 tablespoon olive oil
1 cinnamon stick
2 bay leaves
1 onion, diced
1 teaspoon salt
2 tablespoons ginger purée
2 tablespoons garlic purée
2–3 green chillies, chopped
2½ tablespoons tomato paste (concentrated purée)
1 tablespoon lemon juice
1 tablespoon soft light brown sugar
1 tablespoon ground cumin
1–2 teaspoons chilli powder
1 teaspoon ground coriander
1 teaspoon ground nutmeg
1 teaspoon ground turmeric
1 tablespoon smoked paprika
250ml (9fl oz/1 cup) boiling water
300ml (10½fl oz) double (heavy) cream, plus extra to serve

Combine the black lentils and kidney beans in a bowl and pour over enough room-temperature water to cover by 2.5cm (1in). Leave to soak overnight.

The next day, tip the soaked lentils and beans, along with their soaking water, into a large, heavy casserole pot (Dutch oven). Bring to the boil, then reduce the heat to low and simmer for 1 hour–1 hour 15 minutes until the legumes are soft, stirring occasionally and skimming off any foam that rises to the top.

Drain the softened legumes and allow to cool, then lightly mash them using a potato masher. Set aside while you prepare the masala.

Heat the ghee and oil in a deep heavy-based saucepan over a medium heat. Add the cinnamon stick and bay leaves, and allow them to sizzle for a few minutes and release their aromas. Next, add the onion and salt, then reduce the heat to low and cover with a lid for 5–10 minutes to lightly brown.

Add the ginger, garlic and chilli, then cover with a lid once more and cook for a further 2–4 minutes until very soft. Next add the tomato paste, lemon juice, sugar and ground spices. Cook for another 3–4 minutes, adding a splash of water if needed to prevent the masala from sticking to the bottom.

Once the sourness of the tomato has gone, add the drained legumes, along with the boiling water. Bring to a simmer, cover with the lid once more and cook for 30–40 minutes over a low heat. Add a little oil or ghee if needed to keep it from catching on the bottom of the pan.

Stir in the cream and taste for seasoning, adding salt if needed. Cover once more and simmer for a further 15 minutes until thick, velvety and creamy.

Season to taste, then serve, garnished with a swirl of cream and a little extra ghee.

OVERLEAF *Chicken Makhani and Daal Makhani*

MEHAK'S CHICKEN CURRY

SERVES 4

This is a typical home-style curry. We usually eat it with a salad like the Mango & Feta Kachumber on page 134 and a raita of your choice – I would select the Beetroot Raita on page 163 – along with a butter or garlic naan. This curry is less indulgent than some, but is packed full of flavour and is very hearty. Please feel free to adjust the quantities of chillies and garlic according to your personal preferences.

2½ tablespoons ghee
1 whole mace (nutmeg will work if you can't find mace)
1 tablespoon cumin seeds
1 teaspoon crushed coriander seeds
1 tablespoon freshly ground black pepper
1½ tablespoons garam masala
1 tablespoon ground coriander
1 tablespoon ground turmeric
2 tablespoons garlic purée
2 tablespoons ginger purée
4 green chillies, chopped
2 onions, chopped
6 large tomatoes, roughly chopped
1 tablespoon tomato paste (concentrated purée)
200g (7oz) baby potatoes, peeled
400g (14oz) boneless, skinless chicken thighs, cut into bite-sized chunks
250ml (9fl oz/1 cup) boiling water
sea salt and freshly ground black pepper

TO SERVE
chopped coriander (cilantro)
thumb-sized piece of ginger, chopped into matchsticks
chopped green chillies

Heat the ghee in a deep, heavy-based frying pan over a medium heat. Add the whole spices and cook for 10–20 seconds until they begin to pop. Add the ground spices, along with the garlic, ginger, chillies and onions, and fry for 5 minutes over a low heat.

Blitz the tomatoes in a blender to form a purée, then add this to the pan, along with the tomato paste, potatoes and chicken. Season with a generous pinch of salt and pepper, then increase the heat to medium and cover with a lid. Leave to cook for 20 minutes, stirring occasionally.

Add the boiling water and bring to the boil, then season with salt and pepper to taste once more. Reduce the heat to low and let it simmer and reduce for 20–30 minutes, stirring every now and again.

Serve garnished with coriander, ginger matchsticks and chopped green chillies.

HYDERABADI AUBERGINE

A delicious aubergine curry made with coconut, tamarind and peanut, this is spicy, herbal, sweet, tangy and fragrant.

2 tablespoons mustard oil (use olive oil if you don't have it)
6–8 small Indian (baby) aubergines (eggplants), halved or quartered lengthways, depending on their size
2 red onions, finely sliced
1 tablespoon garlic purée
1 tablespoon ginger purée
1–3 green chillies, depending on how spicy you like it
1 teaspoon cumin seeds
1 teaspoon fennel seeds
1 teaspoon ground turmeric
1 teaspoon chilli powder
400g (14oz) can coconut milk
1 tablespoon tamarind paste
1 tablespoon crunchy peanut butter
1 tablespoon honey (optional, if you want it sweeter)
sea salt and freshly ground black pepper

TO SERVE
handful of coriander (cilantro), chopped
coconut flakes

Heat the oil in a non-stick frying pan over a medium heat. Working in batches, add the aubergines and cook for 3–4 minutes on each side until golden and crispy on the outside and soft and puffy in the middle. Set aside on a plate lined with paper towels while you cook the rest, adding a little more oil if needed.

Once all the aubergines have been cooked and transferred to the plate, add the onion to the now-empty pan and cook for 5–8 minutes until soft and golden. Add the garlic, ginger and chillies, and cook for 1 minute 30 seconds, then add the spices and cook for another 2 minutes.

Tip in the coconut milk, followed by the tamarind, peanut butter and honey (if using). Stir to combine, then simmer gently for 6–8 minutes until the peanut butter is incorporated and the liquid reduces. Return the aubergine to the pan and simmer for 5 minutes.

To serve, stir through the fresh coriander, season to taste and garnish with coconut flakes.

MANGALOREAN CHICKEN

SERVES 4

This dish is a real stunner. With heat from the chillies, sweet nuttiness from the coconut milk and aromatics from the curry leaves, it is layered with different flavours and aromas.

4 tablespoons ghee or olive oil
2 red onions, diced
2 tablespoons garlic purée
2 tablespoons ginger purée
2–4 green chillies, chopped
18 curry leaves (ideally fresh, but dried will do)
1 teaspoon chilli flakes, plus extra to serve
10–15 salted cashews
500g (1lb 2oz) boneless, skinless chicken thighs, chopped into bite-sized chunks
500g (1lb 2oz) skinless chicken drumsticks
400g (14oz) can extra-rich coconut milk
1–2 tablespoons soft light brown sugar
1–2 tablespoons tamarind paste
sea salt and freshly ground black pepper

FOR THE MANGALOREAN SPICE MIX
2 tablespoons coriander seeds
1 tablespoon cumin seeds
1 teaspoon black peppercorns
3 cloves
2.5cm (1in) cinnamon stick
2 dried red chillies
1 teaspoon fennel seeds

To make the Mangalorean spice mix, combine all the spices in a dry frying pan over a low–medium heat and toast for 30 seconds to 1 minute until their aromas are released. Allow to cool, then tip into a spice grinder and blend.

Heat 2 tablespoons of the ghee or oil in the same frying pan over a high heat. Add the freshly ground spice blend and let everything bubble and foam for 20 seconds, then add the onions, garlic and ginger purées and green chillies. Reduce the heat to low and cover with a lid. Cook for 5–8 minutes until the onions go brown and translucent. If the mixture starts to stick to the bottom, add a splash of water or a little ghee.

Meanwhile, heat the remaining 2 tablespoons ghee or olive oil in a large nonstick saucepan over a medium–high heat. Add the curry leaves, chilli flakes and cashews, and allow to sizzle for a minute, then add the chicken to the pan, along with a generous pinch of salt. Sear the chicken for 3 minutes on each side, then transfer the contents of the saucepan to the frying pan with the masala and onions.

Stir in 80ml (2½fl oz/⅓ cup) water and bring to the boil, then cover and cook for 25 minutes, stirring occasionally and making sure it doesn't get too dry (add a splash more water if it does).

Add the coconut milk and sugar, along with ½ tablespoon of the tamarind, and mix well. Bring to the boil, then taste and adjust the seasoning and the tamarind: add salt to taste, more tamarind for extra tang, and more sugar if you would like more sweetness. When you're ready to serve, scatter over some more chilli flakes, if you want a bit more spice.

GOAN CHICKEN & PRAWN SATAY CURRY

SERVES 4–6

This recipe pays homage to the Indian coastline, and Malaysia. This curry is aromatic, sweet, creamy, spicy and moreish. Goan influences can be seen in the spices, and also the richness of the peanut butter, soy sauce and coconut milk.

1 tablespoon olive oil or rapeseed oil
1 large onion, diced
1 tablespoon ginger purée
1 tablespoon garlic purée
2–3 red chillies, chopped
500g (1lb 2oz) boneless, skinless chicken breasts, chopped into bite-sized chunks
1 tablespoon ground cumin
1 teaspoon ground turmeric
1–2 tablespoons smooth peanut butter
100g (3½oz) green beans, trimmed and roughly chopped
400g (14oz) can extra-rich coconut milk
2–3 tablespoons soft light brown sugar
2 tablespoons light soy sauce
2 tablespoons toasted sesame oil
200g (7oz) raw king (jumbo) prawns, peeled, deveined and butterflied
salt

TO SERVE
chopped coriander (cilantro)
chopped red chilli

Heat the oil in a pan over a medium heat. Add the onion, ginger, garlic and chillies, and cook for 5–8 minutes until caramelised and soft. Add the chicken and spices, and cook for another 8–10 minutes.

Stir in the peanut butter, green beans, coconut milk, sugar, soy sauce and sesame oil, and season with a generous pinch of salt. Bring to a slow boil, then reduce the heat to low and let it simmer, blipping gently, for 8 minutes to reduce.

Once the sauce has thickened and reduced, add the prawns and cook for 1 minute until they are pink and cooked through.

Taste and adjust the sugar, salt and soy sauce as needed until that umami note sings.

Garnish with chopped coriander and red chilli, and serve.

KERALAN PRAWNS

SERVES 4–6

This recipe is inspired by the flavours of Kerala in south India, using curry leaves, mustard seeds, tamarind, grated coconut, spices and juicy prawns. The blend of spices here is very different to those found in North Indian dishes.

3 tablespoons olive oil or ghee
1 teaspoon cumin seeds
1 teaspoon mustard seeds
12 fresh curry leaves
1 onion, chopped
1 tablespoon ginger purée
1 tablespoon garlic purée
400g (14oz) can chopped tomatoes
1 teaspoon ground turmeric
1–2 green chillies, finely chopped
1½ tablespoons tamarind paste (alternatively, use a squeeze of lemon juice)
500g (1lb 2oz) raw king (jumbo) prawns, peeled, deveined and butterflied
handful of frozen grated coconut
sea salt

TO SERVE
1 tablespoon runny honey
chopped coriander (cilantro) (optional)

Heat the oil in a deep, heavy-based frying pan over a medium heat. Add the cumin seeds and mustard seeds and allow them to sizzle for 10–20 seconds, then add the curry leaves. Once these are sizzling, add the onion, ginger and garlic, and fry for 3–4 minutes until golden brown.

Once browned, reduce the heat to low and add the tinned tomatoes, turmeric, chillies and tamarind paste. Season with salt, then increase the heat to medium and stir. Cook for 5–8 minutes so the tomatoes and onions melt together, creating a thick masala sauce.

Once the sauce is shiny, add the prawns and coconut, and stir well to coat the prawns in the sauce. Still over a medium heat, cook through for a few minutes until the prawns go pink, being careful not to overcook them.

Drizzle over the honey and garnish with coriander to serve, if you like.

SERVES 4

RED LENTIL CURRY
TADKA DAAL

Tadka means 'to temper', and refers to the tempered spices that top this hearty and flavourful vegetarian dish. You can make this dish vegan by swapping out the ghee for an oil of your choice instead. It is a relatively quick dish to make, but you do need to soak the lentils overnight before you begin.

300g (10½ oz) red lentils
1 tablespoon ground turmeric
handful of chopped coriander (cilantro)
2 tablespoons ghee
sea salt and freshly ground black pepper
chilli powder, to serve (optional)

FOR THE TADKA
2 tablespoons ghee or oil of your choice
2 dried red chillies

1 teaspoon cumin seeds
2 onions, finely sliced
1 tablespoon garlic purée
2 tablespoons ginger purée
1–3 green chillies, chopped
2 large tomatoes, chopped
1 teaspoon ground coriander
1 teaspoon garam masala
1 teaspoon ground turmeric
1 teaspoon smoked paprika

Wash and rinse the lentils, then tip into a bowl and pour over 750ml (26fl oz/3 cups) water. Leave to soak overnight.

The next day, drain the lentils, then tip into a saucepan, along with the turmeric and 375ml (13fl oz/1½ cups) fresh water. Bring to the boil and cook for 5–15 minutes until the lentils have softened and broken down into the water. Take off the heat and set aside.

To make the tadka, heat the ghee or oil in a large, heavy-based pan over a high heat. Once the oil is hot, reduce the heat to medium and add the dried red chillies and cumin seeds. Allow to pop and sizzle for 10–15 seconds, then add the onions, garlic, ginger and chillies. Stir and cook for 5–10 minutes until caramelised.

Add the tomatoes and ground spices, and let it all cook down for another 5 minutes. Once soft, season with a generous pinch of salt, then stir in the cooked lentils.

Season to taste and stir through the coriander. Drizzle over the ghee to finish and serve topped with a dusting of chilli powder (optional).

CHICKPEA CURRY
MASALA CHOLAY

SERVES 4

A hearty, moreish chickpea curry from the north of India, packed full of spices, heat and sweet, tangy tamarind. Absolutely delicious with naans or rice.

2–3 tablespoons ghee
1 cinnamon stick
2 teaspoons cumin seeds
1 teaspoon ajwain seeds
½ teaspoon nigella seeds
2 onions, diced
1 tablespoon garlic purée
2 tablespoons ginger purée
1–3 green chillies, chopped
1 tablespoon garam masala
1 tablespoon ground cumin
1 tablespoon ground turmeric
4 large tomatoes, diced
1kg (2lb 4oz) canned chickpeas (2½ × 400g/14oz cans), rinsed and drained
125ml (4fl oz/½ cup) boiling water
1 tablespoon tamarind paste
pinch of kasoori methi (dried fenugreek leaves)
sea salt and freshly ground black pepper

TO SERVE
handful coriander (cilantro), chopped
thumb-sized piece of ginger, cut into matchsticks (optional)

Heat 1½ tablespoons of the ghee in a deep, heavy-based frying pan over a medium heat. Add the whole dried spices and allow them to sizzle and release their aromas for 10–20 seconds, then add the onions, garlic, ginger and green chillies. Cook for 5 minutes until softened, then add the ground spices, tomatoes, chickpeas and a generous pinch of salt. Cover with a lid and cook for another 5 minutes.

Pour in the boiling water, then stir in the tamarind and kasoori methi. Cover once more and reduce the heat to medium–low. Leave to simmer for 25 minutes, stirring occasionally. If you prefer your curry with more gravy, you can add more boiling water until it reaches your desired consistency.

When the curry is ready, stir through the remaining ghee, season to taste, then serve scattered with coriander and ginger matchsticks, if using.

SERVES 4

KIDNEY BEAN CURRY
RAJMA

Rajma is a red kidney bean curry in a thick gravy base, simmered with whole spices. It is usually served with rice and a dollop of ghee. This dish is regularly eaten throughout Northern India.

- 4 tablespoons ghee or olive oil (or an oil of your choice)
- 1 cardamom pod
- 2 long dried red chillies
- 1 teaspoon cumin seeds
- 1 tablespoon garlic purée
- 2 tablespoons ginger purée
- 2 onions, diced
- 3 fresh tomatoes, diced
- 2 green chillies, finely chopped, plus extra to serve
- 1kg (2lb 4oz) canned kidney beans (2½ × 400g/14oz cans), drained
- 3 tablespoons tomato paste (concentrated purée)
- 1 tablespoon garam masala
- 1 tablespoon ground coriander
- 1 tablespoon ground turmeric
- 1 tablespoon ground cumin
- 1 teaspoon chilli powder
- 1 teaspoon sea salt
- 1 teaspoon freshly ground black pepper
- 375ml (13fl oz/1½ cups) boiling water

TO SERVE
- juice of ½ lemon
- chopped green chillies
- handful of coriander (cilantro), chopped

Heat 3 tablespoons of the ghee or oil in a deep heavy-based saucepan over a medium heat. Once it's hot, add the whole spices and let them cook for 10–20 seconds until they start to sizzle and release their aromas. Add the garlic, ginger, onions, tomatoes and chillies, then cover and cook for 5 minutes until softened.

Add the kidney beans, tomato paste and ground spices. Mix well and stir in the salt and pepper. Cook for another 5 minutes, then add the remaining 1 tablespoon ghee or oil. Cook for 5 minutes more, then pour in the boiling water. Reduce the heat to low and cover. Leave to simmer for 30 minutes until the gravy is thickened and reduced.

When you're ready to serve, season with some more salt and a squeeze of lemon juice. Garnish with green chillies and chopped coriander.

TRADITIONAL EATS

FISH MOILEE

SERVES 4

Moilee is a Goan coconut-based aromatic curry that is layered with curry leaves, lime leaves and mustard seeds. It is usually made with seafood; here, I have used pan-fried sea bass.

4 boneless white fish (such as sea bass) fillets
1 teaspoon ground turmeric
2 teaspoons coconut oil or olive oil
2 teaspoons butter
sea salt and freshly ground black pepper

FOR THE CURRY

2 tablespoons coconut oil or olive oil
1 teaspoon mustard seeds
1 teaspoon fennel seeds
6 fresh curry leaves
4 fresh makrut lime leaves
1 tablespoon garlic purée
1 tablespoon ginger purée
1–3 large red chillies, roughly chopped
1 onion, diced
1 teaspoon garam masala
1 teaspoon ground turmeric, plus extra for dusting
400g (14oz) can extra-rich coconut milk
2 tablespoons soft light brown sugar
zest and juice of 1½ limes
2 spring onions (scallions), chopped

TO SERVE

1 spring onion (scallion), finely chopped
1 red chilli, finely chopped
handful of coriander (cilantro), chopped

Begin by making the curry. Heat the oil in a deep, heavy-based frying pan over a medium heat. Once hot, add the mustard seeds, fennel seeds, curry leaves and makrut lime leaves. Let them pop and sizzle for 10 seconds, then add the garlic, ginger, chillies and onion. Sauté for 5–10 minutes until the onion starts to brown and caramelise.

Add the ground spices and mix well, then stir in the coconut milk, sugar and lime zest. Stir in the juice of 1 lime (save the rest of the juice for the fish) and season with a generous pinch of salt. Reduce the heat to low and let it simmer for 8–10 minutes to reduce and thicken.

Meanwhile, cook the fish. Rub the sea bass fillets with the turmeric, season with salt and pepper, and squeeze over the remaining lime juice. Heat the oil with the butter in a frying pan over a medium heat. Once hot, add the fish fillets, skin-side down, and cook for 5 minutes until the skin is crispy. Turn and cook on the other side for 2 minutes before flipping back.

When everything is ready, stir the spring onions into the curry, then place the fish fillets on top. Garnish with extra spring onion, chilli and coriander to serve.

POTATO & CASHEW CURRY
DUM ALLO CAJU

This recipe is close to my heart, as it takes me back to my childhood memories of India. It is one of those dishes that only the most desi of you will know about – and if you do know it, the very thought of it will make you salivate. This is my version of dum aloo: super-soft baby potatoes encased in a crispy skin, sitting in a spicy yoghurt masala. One taste and you will feel like you are in India, having dinner on the veranda, wrapped up in a cosy shawl.

400g (14oz) baby potatoes, halved
2 tablespoons ghee or olive oil
handful of blanched cashews
1 teaspoon fennel seeds
1 teaspoon cumin seeds
½ teaspoon mustard seeds
1 tablespoon ground turmeric
1 tablespoon tomato paste (concentrated purée)
2 tablespoons garlic purée
1 tablespoon ginger purée
2–3 green bird's-eye chillies, finely chopped
3 tablespoons Greek-style yoghurt
1 teaspoon chilli powder
1 tablespoon freshly ground black pepper
5 tablespoons boiling water
handful of coriander (cilantro), chopped
sea salt

Par-boil the potatoes in a saucepan of boiling water for 15–20 minutes until slightly softened, then drain and allow to cool slightly.

Heat the ghee or oil in a deep, heavy-based frying pan over a medium heat. Once hot, throw in the cashews and whole spices and cook for 10–20 seconds until the seeds pop and release their aromas. Add the turmeric, along with the tomato paste, garlic, ginger and chillies. Stir and cook for 4–5 minutes, then add the potatoes and cook for another 10–12 minutes until softened.

Stir through the yoghurt, chilli powder and black pepper, mixing well. Add the boiling water, along with a pinch of salt and the coriander. Mix well, then take off the heat and allow to stand for 1 minute.

Season to taste, adding more salt and chilli powder if required, then serve.

LAMB & PEA CURRY
KEEMA MUTTAR

SERVES 4

Keema muttar is a spicy lamb and pea curry. Personally, I love to serve this with a Chilli-Cheese Naan (page 148) or Garlic & Coriander Naan (page 149), along with some Green Goddess Chutney (page 156) or Nanima's Tomato Chutney (page 160), and my Classic Kachumber or Mango & Feta Kachumber (both page 134). It is a delicious way to brighten up the flavours and add complexity.

- 2–3 tablespoons ghee, depending on how fatty the mince is
- 1–2 cinnamon sticks
- 2 bay leaves
- 1 teaspoon fennel seeds
- 2 cloves (optional)
- 2–3 dried long red chillies (optional)
- 2 onions, chopped
- 2–3 green chillies, diced (to taste)
- 1 tablespoon garlic purée
- 2 tablespoons ginger purée
- 2 tablespoons tomato paste (concentrated purée)
- 1 tablespoon ground cumin
- 1 teaspoon ground turmeric
- 1 teaspoon ground coriander
- 500g (1lb 2oz) lamb or mutton mince (15–20 per cent fat)
- 130g (4½oz) peas (thawed if using frozen)
- salt

TO SERVE
- handful of chopped coriander (cilantro)
- 1 mild red chilli, sliced
- lemon wedges

Heat the ghee in a heavy based, deep frying pan over a medium–high heat. Once hot, add the cinnamon sticks, bay leaves, fennel seeds, along with the cloves and dried red chillies (if using), and fry for 20 seconds until the aromas are released. Stir in the onions, green chillies, garlic and ginger. Season with a pinch of salt and cover the pan with a lid. Cook for 5–10 minutes until the onions brown, stirring occasionally.

Add the tomato paste and ground spices, then cover once more. Reduce the heat to medium and cook for 5 minutes, then add the mince, along with a pinch of salt. Break up the mince with a spoon, then cover once more and leave to cook for 15 minutes, keeping an eye on it and stirring occasionally so it does not stick to the pan.

Now remove the lid and add in the peas. Let the keema cook down, uncovered, for a further 5–8 minutes until the peas are cooked and tender and the mince has dried up a bit. The texture of the keema should be moist, not too dry and not too wet. Season to taste.

Transfer to your chosen serving dish and garnish with coriander and red chilli slices. Serve with lemon wedges for squeezing.

TOP *Aloo Gobi (page 102)*
BOTTOM *Lamb & Pea Curry*

ALOO GOBI

SERVES 4

You can enjoy this simple potato and cauliflower dish as a main with any of the raitas in Chapter 8 and the Garlic & Coriander Naan on page 149. Alternatively, serve this as a side dish alongside my Daal Makhani (page 81), Rajasthani Lamb Curry (page 78), Lamb & Pea Curry (page 100) or Chicken Makhani (page 80).

- 3 medium potatoes, peeled and cut into bite-sized chunks
- 1 small cauliflower, cut into small florets
- 2 tablespoons olive oil or ghee
- 1 teaspoon cumin seeds
- 1 teaspoon ajwain seeds
- 1 large onion, diced
- 1 tablespoon garlic purée
- 1 tablespoon ginger purée
- 2 green bird's-eye chillies, chopped
- 2 tomatoes, diced
- 1 teaspoon ground turmeric
- 1 teaspoon ground cumin
- ½ teaspoon ground coriander
- ½ teaspoon smoked paprika
- 1 teaspoon garam masala
- juice of ½ lemon
- handful of coriander (cilantro), chopped
- salt

Bring a large saucepan of salted water to the boil. Add the potatoes and cauliflower and boil for 15–20 minutes until soft but not cooked all the way through. Drain and leave to steam dry in the colander.

Heat the olive oil or ghee in a frying pan over a medium heat. Once hot, add the cumin seeds and ajwain seeds, and allow them to pop and sizzle for 10–15 seconds. Add the onion, garlic, ginger and chillies, along with a pinch of salt. Cover the pan with a lid and leave to cook for 6–8 minutes until browned and caramelised.

Now add the tomatoes and ground spices and mix well. Cover once more and cook for a further 5 minutes until the tomatoes release their juices and soften. If the mixture is starting to stick to the pan, add a splash of hot water or a little more oil/ghee to help loosen the masala.

Add the par-boiled potatoes and cauliflower and stir well to combine. Reduce the heat to low and cover once more. Cook for a further 10–12 minutes until the vegetables are soft, then season to taste and stir in the lemon juice and fresh coriander.

Serve in your favourite dish and enjoy.

AUBERGINE BARTHA

SERVES 4

This is one of my favourite dishes, and I believe most continents have their own version of this charred, fleshy aubergine dish. Bartha is made with spices, tomatoes and onions, cooked down to a delicious dish that is perfect with naans or roti.

- 2 aubergines (eggplants)
- 2 tablespoons olive oil or rapeseed oil
- 1 tablespoon cumin seeds
- 2 onions, diced
- 1½ tablespoons garlic purée
- 1 tablespoon ginger purée
- 2–3 green chillies, chopped
- 1½ teaspoons ground turmeric
- 1 tablespoon ground coriander
- 1 teaspoon garam masala
- 2 tablespoons tomato paste (concentrated purée)
- 200g (7oz) cherry tomatoes, sliced
- 1 teaspoon sea salt
- handful of coriander (cilantro), chopped (if you don't like coriander, use parsley instead)
- squeeze of lemon juice (optional)

Begin by roasting your aubergines. The best way to do this is to carefully hold them over a gas flame using a pair of tongs, turning until the skin is scorched and charred. This can take 10–18 minutes, depending on the size and freshness of your aubergines. If you do not have a gas hob, you can preheat your oven to 170°C (325°F/gas mark 3), then prick the aubergines with a fork, rub them with oil, wrap them in foil and roast for 30–45 minutes.

Once roasted/scorched, peel away and discard the skins, then chop the flesh and set aside.

Heat the oil in a heavy-based frying pan over a medium heat. Once it's hot, throw in the cumin seeds and let them sizzle and pop for 10 seconds. Next add the onions, garlic, ginger and chillies, and cook for 5–10 minutes until super soft and brown.

Add the aubergine flesh, along with the ground spices, tomato paste and cherry tomatoes, and season with the salt. Cover with a lid and cook for 5–10 minutes until the tomatoes blister, soften and burst.

Once everything looks soft and delicious, taste for seasoning and add more salt if required, then scatter over the coriander or parsley, add a squeeze of lemon, if using, and enjoy!

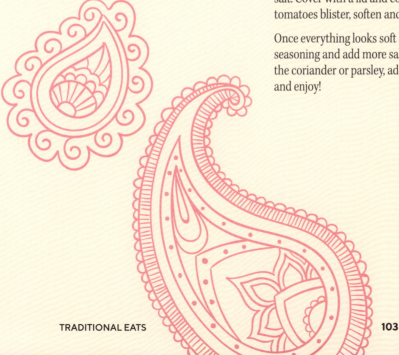

TRADITIONAL EATS

KARAHI PANEER

I like to serve this with my Plain Naan (page 144), Beetroot & Chickpea Salad (page 138) and Caramelised Garlic Raita (page 167).

- 2 tablespoons ghee or olive oil, plus extra to serve (optional)
- 1 teaspoon cumin seeds
- 1 teaspoon fennel seeds
- 2 long dried red chillies
- 1 onion, cut into chunks
- 3 green chillies, chopped
- 1½ tablespoons garlic purée
- 1½ tablespoons ginger purée
- 2 tablespoons tomato paste (concentrated purée)
- 1–2 tablespoons soft light brown sugar
- 1 teaspoon ground turmeric
- 1 tablespoon garam masala
- 1 teaspoon ground coriander
- 1 teaspoon chilli powder
- 400g (14oz) paneer, cut into cubes
- 2 green bell peppers (capsicums), cut into chunks
- splash of boiling water
- 2–3 tablespoons Greek-style yoghurt
- 1 tablespoon kasoori methi (dried fenugreek leaves)
- chopped coriander (cilantro), to serve
- salt

Heat the ghee in a large karahi or wok-style pan over a medium–high heat. Once hot, reduce the heat to medium and add the cumin seeds, fennel seeds and dried red chillies. Let them pop and sizzle for 15 seconds, then add the onion, green chilli, garlic and ginger, and cook for 5–7 minutes until the onion begins to brown a little.

Stir in the tomato paste, along with the sugar and ground spices. Season with a generous pinch of salt, then cook for another 6–8 minutes.

Add the paneer and green peppers and stir to coat really well. Add the boiling water and cook for 6–8 minutes until the paneer is soft and the peppers are tender.

Stir in the Greek yoghurt, then reduce the heat to low and cook for a further 3–5 minutes.

Season to taste, adding more salt or sugar if needed, then stir in the kasoori methi. If you like, you can stir through another spoonful of ghee just before serving.

Garnish with coriander and serve.

SEASONAL SAAG

SERVES 4–6

Saag is a dish that is always prepared during the harvest season in North India. The air would be filled with the aroma of mustard greens being cooked in copious amounts of ghee and spices. Saag is a dish I often crave, but it is very hard to get hold of mustard greens. Instead, this recipe uses kale and baby spinach.

500g (1lb 2oz) frozen chopped kale (or 400g/14oz fresh)
500g (1lb 2oz) baby leaf spinach
2 large white onions, chopped
2 tablespoons garlic purée
2½ tablespoons ginger purée
2 tomatoes, chopped
2–3 green bird's eye chillies, chopped
3–4 tablespoons ghee
1 teaspoon cumin seeds
1 whole mace
1 teaspoon ajwain seeds
2 dried long red Kashmiri chillies
1 tablespoon ground cumin
1 teaspoon garam masala
½ teaspoon ground turmeric
125ml (4fl oz/½ cup) single (pure) cream, plus extra to serve
salt and freshly ground black pepper

TO SERVE
1 teaspoon salted butter
small handful of coriander (cilantro)

Fill a large saucepan with water and bring to the boil. Add the kale and boil for a few minutes until it darkens and wilts, then drain and tip into a blender. Add the baby spinach, onions, garlic, ginger, tomatoes and chillies to the blender, along with 125ml (4fl oz/½ cup) water. Blend until the mixture is smooth and slightly loose.

Melt the ghee in a heavy-based frying pan over a medium heat. Once hot, add the cumin seeds, mace, ajwain seeds and dried red chillies. Let them sizzle and pop for 10–15 seconds until their aromas are released, then add the ground spices, along with the kale and spinach purée. Stir well, reduce the heat to low–medium, and cook for 10–15 minutes.

Once the purée starts to thicken a little, add the cream, season to taste and take off the heat. The texture should be thick and velvety.

Swirl through the salted butter and a little extra cream to serve, then scatter with the coriander and enjoy.

MUTTON CURRY
SALI BOTI

SERVES 4–6

This is a Parsi mutton dish topped with potato sticks.

1kg (2lb 4oz) lamb or mutton shoulder, chopped into bite-sized chunks
4–5 tablespoons olive oil
2 cinnamon sticks
3–4 dried bay leaves
1 teaspoon cumin seeds
1 teaspoon ajwain seeds
2 green cardamom pods
2–3 green bird's-eye chillies, chopped
2½ onions, chopped
2½ tablespoons tomato paste (concentrated purée)
1½ tablespoons garam masala

FOR THE MARINADE
130g (4½ oz/½ cup) plain yoghurt
2 tablespoons garlic purée
2 tablespoons ginger purée
1 tablespoon chilli powder
1½ tablespoons ground coriander
1 teaspoon ground turmeric
1½ teaspoons salt
2 tablespoons olive oil

TO SERVE
handful of chopped coriander (cilantro)
handful of shoestring potato fries/potato sticks (shop-bought – see tip)
Plain Naans (page 144)
steamed basmati rice

In a large mixing bowl, combine the marinade ingredients. Add the meat and stir to coat, then transfer to the refrigerator and leave to marinate for 30 minutes.

When you're ready to cook, heat the oil in a heavy-based frying pan or karahi over a medium–high heat. Once hot, reduce the heat to medium and add the cinnamon sticks, bay leaves, cumin seeds, ajwain seeds, cardamom pods, green chillies and onions. Cook for 8–10 minutes until the onions have browned and softened, stirring occasionally, then add the tomato paste and cook for a further 5–6 minutes.

Now add the marinated meat, along with the garam masala. The meat will start to brown and release its juices. Season with salt, then cover and reduce the heat to low. Cook for 1 hour–1 hour 15 minutes, checking on the dish halfway through to ensure it is not catching at the bottom. If it is catching, stir in a splash of water to loosen.

By this time, the meat should be tender and cooked through. Increase the heat to high so the oil starts to bubble its way to the top of the curry. Once this happens, it is ready to eat.

Serve topped with coriander and shoestring potato fries, with naans and rice on the side.

TIP *If you are not able to buy ready-made potato sticks/shoestring fries, then simply slice ¼ potato into thin strips and shallow-fry for 5–6 minutes until golden and crisp. Set aside on a plate lined with paper towels to drain any excess oil.*

RESHMI CHICKEN CURRY

SERVES 4–5

You may not be familiar with this curry, but if you like kormas and similar dishes, you will love this: it is mildly spiced, aromatic, creamy, herbal and moreish. It's also easy to cook.

2–3 tablespoons ghee
650g (1lb 7oz) boneless, skinless chicken breasts, cut into bite-sized chunks
1 tablespoon ginger purée
1½ tablespoons garlic purée
1 teaspoon salt
200g (7oz/¾ cup) plain yoghurt, lightly whisked
1 tablespoon ground cumin
1 teaspoon chilli powder
1 teaspoon freshly ground black pepper
1 teaspoon ground nutmeg
250ml (9fl oz/1 cup) double (heavy) cream
150g (5½oz) grated mozzarella

TO SERVE
chopped coriander (cilantro)
sliced spring onions (scallions)
Garlic & Coriander Naans (page 149)

Melt the ghee in a heavy-based frying pan over a medium heat. Once hot, add the chicken, along with the ginger and garlic purées and the salt. Cook for 6–8 minutes until starting to brown, then reduce the heat to low, add the yoghurt and cook for 1 minute more.

Turn the heat back to medium and add the spices. Cook for a further 6–8 minutes until the ghee rises to the top, then stir in the cream. Cook for 2 minutes, then add the mozzarella and cook for 2 minutes more.

Divide between bowls, scatter with coriander and spring onions, and enjoy with garlic naans.

TRADITIONAL EATS

GRILLS

I am sure that this chapter will soon be a firm favourite in your kitchen, and I predict many bookmarks and folded page corners.

All the recipes here are easy, accessible and full of flavour. Some can be cooked in a hurry; others deserve to be given a little more time and love to marinate.

Cook them in your oven, on a barbecue or under a grill, and pair them with your favourite salads, naans, chutneys and raitas, or simply serve with some steamed basmati rice.

LAHORI KARAHI CHICKEN TIKKA

If you love deeply flavoured curried chicken, but want minimal fuss and a dish that doesn't require babysitting, this recipe is for you. The secret to this simple curry is to brown off the onions, garlic, ginger and chilli beforehand with the mace and cumin seeds, then throw them into an oven dish with the rest of the ingredients. I like to serve this with Plain Naans (page 144) or Garlic & Coriander Naans (page 149). Enjoy!

- 650g (1lb 7oz) boneless, skinless chicken thighs, chopped into halves
- 1½ teaspoons ground turmeric
- 1½ teaspoons garam masala
- 1 teaspoon ground nutmeg
- 1 teaspoon ground coriander
- 1 tablespoon Kashmiri chilli powder
- 3–4 tablespoons lemon juice, or 2 tablespoons white wine vinegar
- 4 tablespoons Greek-style yoghurt
- 1 onion, sliced
- thumb-sized piece of ginger, cut into matchsticks, to serve
- sea salt and freshly ground black pepper

FOR THE BROWNED ONIONS
- 2 tablespoons ghee
- 1 teaspoon cumin seeds
- 1 whole mace
- 2 onions, sliced
- 2 tablespoons ginger purée
- 3 tablespoons garlic purée
- 2 red chillies, diced
- 1 green chilli, diced
- small pinch of sugar

FOR THE BLITZED HERBS
- bunch of coriander (cilantro)
- bunch of mint, leaves picked
- 1½ tablespoons olive oil or rapeseed oil

Preheat the oven to 200°C (400°F/gas mark 6).

Begin by preparing the browned onions. Heat the ghee in a frying pan over a medium heat. Add the cumin seeds and mace, and let them fizz and pop for 1 minute, then add the onions, ginger, garlic and chillies. Season with the sugar and a pinch of salt. Let them slowly cook for 10 minutes until brown, then set aside.

To make the blitzed herbs, combine the coriander, mint leaves and oil in a blender. Blitz to form a purée and season with a little salt.

In a large mixing bowl, combine the chicken with all the remaining ingredients except the sliced onion and ginger matchsticks. Add the browned onions and two-thirds of the blitzed herbs and stir well to combine, then transfer to a roasting tray. Throw the sliced onion over the top and season generously with salt and pepper.

Roast for 30–35 minutes until the chicken is cooked through and slightly charred on top.

Serve with the remaining blitzed herbs and the ginger matchsticks.

SIMPLE CHICKEN TIKKA

This is an easy-peasy chicken tikka recipe that you can simply throw together and pop into the oven with minimal fuss: perfect for a midweek family dinner. I would recommend serving this with Apple Raita (page 166), Plain Naan (page 144) and Sweet Potato Tabbouleh (page 136).

650–700g (1lb 7oz–1lb 9oz) boneless, skinless chicken thighs, chopped into bite-sized pieces
2 tablespoons full-fat Greek-style yoghurt
2 tablespoons tomato paste (concentrated purée)
2 tablespoons ghee
2 tablespoons garlic purée
2 tablespoons ginger purée
3 green bird's-eye chillies, finely chopped
1 tablespoon ground turmeric
1 teaspoon ground coriander
1 tablespoon ground cumin
1 tablespoon smoked paprika
1 teaspoon garam masala
zest and juice of 1 lime
2 red onions, finely sliced
2 long red Romano peppers, sliced, or 200g (7oz) mini red bell pepper (capsicum)
olive oil, for drizzling
2½ tablespoons runny honey
handful of coriander (cilantro), chopped
sea salt

Preheat the oven to 170°C (325°F/gas mark 3).

In a bowl, combine the chicken with the yoghurt, tomato paste, ghee, garlic, ginger, chillies, ground spices and lime zest and juice. Mix well, then tip into a baking tray. Scatter the onions and peppers over the top, then drizzle with the olive oil and honey. Season with salt and bake for 15–20 minutes, then give it all a mix and bake for another 15 minutes.

The chicken should be cooked through, and the onions and peppers should be blistered and caramelised.

Scatter over the fresh coriander and serve with your chosen accompaniments.

AFGHANI CHICKEN TIKKA

SERVES 4

This Afghani-style chicken tikka is made with a creamier and more peppery and herbal marinade; traditionally it would be made with a cashew butter or cream, and poppy seeds would also be used.

- 8 boneless, skinless chicken thighs, chopped into bite-sized pieces
- 3 tablespoons kasoori methi (dried fenugreek leaves)
- 1½ tablespoons garlic purée
- 1½ tablespoons ginger purée
- 1½ tablespoons chilli powder
- 1 teaspoon pink Himalayan salt (regular salt is fine if you don't have it)
- 1½ tablespoons ground turmeric
- 1 tablespoon freshly ground black pepper
- ½ tablespoon ground cinnamon
- 5 green chillies, chopped
- 250g (9oz) Greek-style yoghurt
- 2 red onions, finely sliced
- 1 tablespoon olive oil
- sea salt

Preheat the oven to 200°C (400°F/gas mark 6).

Simply combine the chicken in a large bowl with all the ingredients except the onions and olive oil. Mix well, then tip into a baking tray. Scatter the onions on top and drizzle over the olive oil. Season with salt, then roast for 25 minutes. That's it – ready to serve!

SERVES 4-6

MALAI CHICKEN TIKKA

I'm sure this marinade will soon become one of your go-tos. Here, I have used chicken, but it is also delicious over salmon, paneer, mushrooms or potatoes. This dish is perfect served with the naan of your choice, alongside my Beetroot & Chickpea Salad (page 138) and some Green Goddess Chutney (page 156).

700g (1lb 7oz) boneless, skinless chicken thighs, chopped into bite-sized chunks

FOR THE MARINADE
2 tablespoons tomato paste (concentrated purée)
handful of coriander (cilantro), chopped, plus extra to serve
3 green bird's-eye chillies, chopped
3 tablespoons kasoori methi (dried fenugreek leaves)
3 tablespoons garlic purée
2 tablespoons ginger purée
1½ teaspoons ground turmeric
2 tablespoons ghee, melted, plus extra for drizzling
2 tablespoons olive oil, plus extra for drizzling
1 tablespoon ground cumin
1 tablespoon salt
1 teaspoon freshly ground black pepper
1 tablespoon chilli powder
300g (10½oz) cream cheese

In a mixing bowl, combine all the marinade ingredients. The ingredients may be a little difficult to mix; you can either use a spatula or put on some food-preparation gloves and use your hands to mix them.

Once combined, add the chicken and stir well to coat. Leave to marinate in the refrigerator for at least 2–3 hours, preferably overnight.

When you're ready to cook, preheat your oven to 170°C (325°F/gas mark 3).

Transfer the marinated chicken into a baking tray or ovenproof dish. Drizzle over a little melted ghee or oil of your choice, then bake for 30–35 minutes, turning after 15 minutes to ensure the chicken is cooked on both sides.

Once the chicken is cooked through, serve with your chosen accompaniments, garnished with a little coriander if you wish.

SERVES 4–6

CHIPOTLE SALMON TIKKA

This dish is best served with the naan of your choice, along with my Mango & Feta Kachumber (page 134) and Grilled Pineapple Chutney (page 157) or Green Goddess Chutney (page 156).

4–6 salmon fillets, skin on (about 500g/1lb 2oz)
2 tablespoons oil of your choice or melted ghee

FOR THE MARINADE
1 onion, roughly chopped
4 tablespoons full-fat Greek-style yoghurt
1 tablespoon chipotle paste
2 tablespoons tomato paste (concentrated purée)
1 tablespoon smoked paprika
1 teaspoon salt
1 teaspoon freshly ground black pepper
1 tablespoon ginger purée
1½ tablespoons garlic purée
1–2 red chillies, chopped
1 teaspoon ground turmeric
juice of ½ lemon
1 tablespoon soft dark brown sugar

TO SERVE
dried chilli flakes
handful of coriander (cilantro), chopped
lime wedges

Begin by blitzing the onion in a blender to form a purée. Add this to a mixing bowl, along with all the other marinade ingredients, and mix well.

Add the salmon and turn to coat, then leave to marinate in the refrigerator for at least 2–3 hours, preferably overnight.

When you're ready to cook, preheat your oven to 160°C (315°F/gas mark 2–3). Transfer the marinated salmon into a baking tray or ovenproof dish. Drizzle with the melted ghee or oil, then cook for 20–25 minutes, basting the salmon after about 10 minutes.

Once the salmon is cooked through, serve it with your chosen accompaniments, garnished with chilli flakes and coriander, with lime wedges for squeezing.

GRILLS

HARISSA PANEER TIKKA

SERVES 4–6

This recipe combines classic Moroccan and Indian spices to create a delicious marinade that is full of flavour. This dish is best served with any naan of your choice, along with my Sweet Potato Tabbouleh (page 136), Cucumber & Mint Raita (page 164) and Hot Hummus (page 26). This combination will give you a real Indo-Persian/Moroccan spread full of fresh flavours, with layers and layers of complexity in each bite.

600g (1lb 5oz) paneer, cut into large, flat cubes
2 green bell peppers (capsicums), cut into chunks
1 onion, sliced
olive oil or ghee, for drizzling

FOR THE MARINADE
2 tablespoons full-fat Greek yoghurt
1 tablespoon harissa paste
1 tablespoon ginger purée
1½ tablespoons garlic purée
1 tablespoon date molasses
1 teaspoon smoked paprika, plus extra to serve
1 teaspoon ground turmeric
1 teaspoon salt
1 teaspoon freshly ground black pepper

TO SERVE
handful of chopped coriander (cilantro)
lime wedges

In a mixing bowl, combine all the marinade ingredients and mix well. Add the paneer and stir to coat in the marinade. Cover and leave to marinate for at least 2–3 hours in the refrigerator, preferably overnight.

When you're ready to cook, preheat your oven to 160°C (315°F/gas mark 2–3).

Tip the marinated paneer into an ovenproof dish, then scatter the green peppers and onion over the top. Drizzle a little melted ghee or olive oil over the paneer and bake for 15–20 minutes.

Once cooked, scatter with the coriander and serve with lime wedges for squeezing.

KALI MIRCH CHICKEN TIKKA

This is a black pepper chicken tikka, made with cream cheese, spices and black pepper.

550g (1lb 4oz) skinless, boneless chicken breasts, cut into bite-sized pieces

FOR THE MARINADE

250g (9oz) full-fat cream cheese
1–2 tablespoons melted ghee, plus extra to serve
1 tablespoon garlic purée
2 green bird's-eye chillies, finely chopped
1 teaspoon ground green cardamom
1½ teaspoons garam masala
1 teaspoon coarsely ground black pepper
1 teaspoon ground white pepper
1½ teaspoons salt

TO SERVE

1 tablespoon melted ghee (optional)
chaat masala, for dusting
handful of finely chopped coriander (cilantro) or parsley
lemon or lime wedges

Combine the marinade ingredients in a mixing bowl and mix well. Add the chicken and stir to coat, then cover and leave to marinate in the refrigerator for 1–2 hours.

Preheat the oven to 180°C (350°F/gas mark 4) and line a baking tray with foil.

When you're ready to cook, arrange the marinated chicken on the prepared baking tray. Roast for 25–30 minutes, turning halfway through and basting the meat with its own juices.

Once the chicken is cooked through and slightly charred around the edges, remove it from the oven and transfer to a serving dish. Drizzle over some extra ghee, if using, dust with chaat masala, then scatter over the coriander or parsley and serve with lemon or lime wedges for squeezing.

PORTOBELLO MUSHROOM TIKKA

SERVES 4-6

Meaty portobellos marinated in a masala that clings on to the mushrooms and injects them with a real hit of flavour. These mushrooms are perfect when you want a veg to be the star of the show. They are delicious served with Chilli-Cheese Naans (page 148) and Green Goddess Chutney (page 156) or Chilli Garlic Pesto (page 161).

6 large portobello mushrooms

FOR THE MARINADE
5 tablespoons full-fat cream cheese
1 tablespoon ginger purée
1 tablespoon garlic purée
2 tablespoons olive oil
1 tablespoon smoked paprika
1 teaspoon chilli powder
1 teaspoon ground turmeric
3 green chillies, finely chopped
1 tablespoon onion powder
1 tablespoon garam masala
1 teaspoon salt

TO SERVE
chaat masala, for dusting
handful of chopped dill
handful of chopped chives
lemon or lime wedges

In a mixing bowl, combine all the marinade ingredients and mix well. Add the mushrooms and turn to coat in the marinade. Leave to marinate at room temperature for 30 minutes or in the refrigerator for 1–2 hours.

When you're ready to cook, preheat your oven to 170°C (325°F/gas mark 3) and line a large baking tray with foil.

Arrange the marinated mushrooms on the prepared baking tray, spreading them out and ensuring there are gaps between them; you don't want the tray to be overcrowded or the mushrooms to be stacked on top of each other.

Roast for 30–35 minutes.

Transfer the mushrooms and their juices to a serving dish. Dust with the chaat masala, sprinkle over the dill and chives, and serve with lemon or lime wedges for squeezing.

GRILLS

LAMB CHOP TIKKA

If, like me, you love lamb chops marinated in a spicy masala, you will love this dish. The marinade tenderises the meat, and it becomes so juicy that this will surely be a recipe you want to cook over and over again. I love to serve this with my Cumin Cretan Salad (page 141), Sweet Potato Tabbouleh (page 136) and Caramelised Garlic Raita (page 167).

800g (1lb 12 oz) lamb chops

FOR THE MARINADE
4 tablespoons full-fat Greek-style yoghurt
1 tablespoon ginger purée
1 tablespoon garlic purée
1 tablespoon lemon juice
2 tablespoons olive oil
1 tablespoon smoked paprika
1 teaspoon chilli powder
1 teaspoon ground turmeric
1½ teaspoons ajwain seeds
1 teaspoon ground cinnamon
1 teaspoon ground cumin
2 tablespoons dried tarragon
1 tablespoon chilli flakes (optional)
1 teaspoon salt

TO SERVE
chaat masala, for dusting
handful of chopped coriander (cilantro)
lemon or lime wedges

In a mixing bowl, combine all the marinade ingredients and mix well. Add the lamb chops and turn to coat in the marinade. Leave to marinate at room temperature for 30 minutes or in the refrigerator for 1–2 hours, or preferably overnight.

When you're ready to cook, preheat your oven to 200°C (400°F/gas mark 6) and line a large baking tray with foil.

Arrange the marinated lamb chops on the prepared baking tray, spreading them out and ensuring there are gaps between them; you don't want the tray to be overcrowded or the chops to be stacked on top of each other. Cover the chops with a layer of foil; this is essential to keep in the moisture and stop the meat from drying out.

Add to the oven and cook for 20–30 minutes, then remove the foil and baste the chops with their own juices. Cook, uncovered, for a further 20–30 minutes until cooked through.

Transfer the chops and their cooking juices to a serving dish. Dust with chaat masala and scatter over the coriander. Serve with lemon or lime wedges, for squeezing.

FISH TIKKA

You will need a meaty fish for this recipe so that the fish retains its texture and the masala doesn't overpower it. Serve this with my Cumin Cretan Salad (page 141) and Grilled Pineapple Chutney (page 157).

500g (1lb 2oz) cod loin or salmon, cut into 4cm (1½in) pieces
lime wedges, to serve

FOR THE MARINADE

2 tablespoons olive oil or melted ghee
4 tablespoons Greek-style yoghurt
1 tablespoon ginger purée
2 tablespoons garlic purée
zest and juice of 1 lime
1 teaspoon ground turmeric
1 teaspoon ground cumin
1½ teaspoons chilli flakes
1 teaspoon ajwain seeds
½ teaspoon chilli powder
1 tablespoon kasoori methi (dried fenugreek leaves)
handful of freshly chopped dill, plus extra to serve
1½ teaspoons salt

In a mixing bowl, combine all the marinade ingredients. Add the fish pieces, and turn to coat in the marinade. Leave to marinate for 20 minutes at room temperature.

Preheat the oven to 170°C (325°F/gas mark 3) and line a baking tray with foil.

Arrange the marinated fish pieces on the prepared tray, spacing them well out. If there is skin on the fish, then place the pieces skin-side down.

Roast for 8–10 minutes, or until the fish has turned opaque and is cooked through.

Scatter over some dill and serve with lime wedges for squeezing.

CHAPALI LAMB OR CHICKEN KEBABS

SERVES 4–6

Here, I've given you the option of shallow-frying the kebabs or grilling them on skewers. You can choose between lamb or chicken. If you want to give your kebabs an additional hit of flavour, add a piece of mozzarella or mild Cheddar cheese to the middle of each one.

1 onion, finely diced

FOR THE LAMB CHAPALI KEBAB

650g (1lb 7oz) lamb mince (20 per cent fat)
1 tomato, deseeded and finely diced
2 green bird's-eye chillies, finely diced
1 tablespoon ginger purée
1 teaspoon garlic purée
1 teaspoon fennel seeds
1 teaspoon ground coriander
1 teaspoon ground cumin
1 tablespoon gram flour (also known as chickpea or besan flour) or plain (all-purpose) flour
olive oil, for drizzling or shallow-frying

FOR THE CHICKEN CHAPALI KEBAB

650g (1lb 7oz) chicken mince
1 tomato, deseeded and finely diced
2 green bird's-eye chillies, finely diced
1 tablespoon ginger purée
1 teaspoon garlic purée
1 teaspoon smoked paprika
1 teaspoon garam masala
1 teaspoon dried tarragon
1 tablespoon gram flour (also known as chickpea or besan flour) or plain (all-purpose) flour
olive oil, for drizzling or shallow-frying

OVERLEAF *Chapali Lamb or Chicken Kebabs, with Garlic and Coriander Naan (page 149), Classic Kachumber (page 134) and Cucumber and Mint Raita (page 164).*

Wrap the chopped onion in a muslin cloth and squeeze to remove the excess water. It is important to do this, as the moisture can interfere with the texture of the kebab, making it loose, or causing it to split while cooking.

Tip the squeezed onion into a mixing bowl. Add all the remaining ingredients for your chosen kebab, except the oil, and mix well using your hands until everything is well combined and the mixture is starting to stick to your fingers.

TO SHALLOW-FRY:

Divide the mixture into six equal portions and shape these into round patties that are flatter than a burger.

Heat 4 tablespoons olive oil in a heavy-based frying pan over a medium heat. Once hot, add the kebabs and shallow-fry for 10–12 minutes, turning halfway through. Before you turn them, it is important to ensure that the side that is cooking has turned golden and has a brown crust; when both sides have this, you know the kebab is cooked.

Serve.

TO GRILL ON SKEWERS:

If you prefer, you can shape these kebabs around soaked bamboo skewers, pressing the mixture on to the skewers and shaping it into long kebabs.

Line a baking tray with foil and place a wire rack inside the tray so the fat and oil can drip down on to the tray. Drizzle a little olive oil over the kebabs and cook under a hot grill for 7 minutes on each side. You want slight char marks on the kebabs from the rack they are cooking on, and they should be a little crispy on the outside.

Serve with Garlic and Coriander Naan (page 149), Classic Kachumber (page 134) and Cucumber and Mint Raita (page 164).

GRILLS

SALADS

This chapter is full of delicious, zingy and easy salads that you can prepare in very little time.

I draw on influences from Greece, Mexico, India and the Middle East to show you how versatile flavours can be.

MANGO & FETA KACHUMBER

SERVES 4–5

This is a great light, refreshing, zingy, salty, sweet and punchy salad that is perfect as a side, as a main or paired with anything from the grills section. I've included the option of using tajín, a Mexican seasoning that brings a blend of citrus and salty spice, which is well worth including if you can source it.

- 2 large ripe mangoes, peeled, pitted and chopped into bite-sized chunks
- 150g (5½ oz) feta, crumbled
- 1 cucumber, chopped into bite-sized chunks
- ½ red onion, finely sliced
- 1 large red chilli, finely chopped
- handful of mint, chopped
- zest and juice of 1 lime
- 2 tablespoons olive oil
- ½ teaspoon tajín (optional)
- salt

In a mixing bowl, simply combine all the ingredients and mix well, but be gentle – you don't want to bruise the mango or overwork the feta so it starts to disintegrate. Season to taste with salt and serve.

CLASSIC KACHUMBER

SERVES 4

The most widely eaten salad in India, the classic kachumber is a holy trinity mix of cucumber, tomatoes and onions. This recipe has pomegranate as well, which adds delicious bursts of tart sweetness to each mouthful.

- 1 small red onion, finely chopped
- 1 large cucumber, chopped into small cubes
- 3 ripe tomatoes, chopped into small pieces
- handful of pomegranate seeds (optional)

FOR THE DRESSING
- handful of coriander (cilantro), chopped
- 1 green bird's-eye chilli, finely chopped
- zest and juice of 2 limes
- ½ teaspoon chaat masala
- salt and freshly ground black pepper

Simply combine the onion, cucumber, tomatoes and pomegranate seeds in your salad bowl. Add the dressing ingredients directly to the salad bowl and toss well.

Season to taste and enjoy!

SWEET POTATO TABBOULEH

SERVES 4

This is my take on the classic Middle Eastern salad, using deliciously spiced sweet potatoes to give it more flavour and dimension.

2–3 sweet potatoes, peeled
80g (2¾oz) bulgur wheat
2 handfuls of parsley, chopped
handful of mint, chopped
1 red onion, finely diced
6 dried apricots, chopped into small pieces
½ cucumber, chopped into small chunks

FOR THE DRESSING
juice of 3–4 lemons
½ teaspoon chilli flakes
1 garlic clove, grated, or 1 teaspoon garlic purée
½ teaspoon ground coriander
4 tablespoons olive oil
2 tablespoons maple syrup or agave syrup
salt

Bring a saucepan of water to the boil. Add the sweet potatoes and boil for 15–20 minutes until soft, then drain and set aside to cool. Once cool, chop into small chunks.

Tip the bulgur wheat into a separate saucepan and add enough cold water to half-fill the pan. Bring to the boil, then cook for 15–20 minutes until cooked through. Drain any excess water using a sieve and set aside to cool.

Once cool, add the sweet potato and bulgur wheat to a salad bowl, along with the fresh herbs, onion, apricots and cucumber.

In a small bowl, combine all the dressing ingredients and season to taste with salt. Pour the dressing over the salad and toss to combine. Adjust the seasoning if needed, and enjoy.

BEETROOT & CHICKPEA SALAD

SERVES 3–4

An easy salad that comes together in no time at all, this is packed full of goodness with beetroots and chickpeas dressed in a light, sweet, zingy and herby dressing.

4 raw beetroots, peeled and cut into wedges
400g (14oz) can chickpeas, rinsed and drained
3 tablespoons olive oil
½ teaspoon ajwain seeds
½ teaspoon fennel seeds
2 carrots, peeled and grated
handful of dill, chopped
handful of coriander (cilantro), chopped
2 handfuls of baby spinach
2 spring onions (scallions), chopped
salt

FOR THE DRESSING
zest and juice of 1 large orange
2 tablespoons red wine vinegar
2–3 tablespoons olive oil
1 tablespoon maple syrup or agave syrup
1 tablespoon garlic purée
⅓ teaspoon chilli powder

TO SERVE (OPTIONAL)
small handful of crushed walnuts
50g (1¾oz) feta, crumbled, or Parmesan, grated

Preheat the oven to 180°C (350°F/gas mark 4). Line a baking tray with baking parchment.

Tip the beetroot wedges and chickpeas into the prepared tray and spread them out. Drizzle over the oil, then scatter over the ajwain and fennel seeds. Season with salt and roast for 20–25 minutes until the beetroots are just softened but still a little firm. Remove from the oven and set aside to cool.

Once cool, tip into a salad bowl and add the carrots, fresh herbs, spinach and spring onions.

In a separate bowl, combine all the dressing ingredients and mix well. Pour the dressing over the salad and toss to combine. Season to taste and garnish with the walnuts and cheese, if using.

SERVES 4

CUMIN CRETAN SALAD

This has to be my all-time favourite salad; it is a variation of the famous Greek salad, and is widely eaten in Crete. The traditional version uses a fresh cheese called mizithra; if you like, you can use feta, as this is closest in taste, but my recipe uses a whole burrata for its creamy texture, which provides a delicious contrast with the herby, spicy dressing.

2 slices of crusty sourdough
olive oil, for drizzling
3 tomatoes, chopped
15 black Kalamata olives
1 red onion, diced
½ cucumber, chopped
handful of dill, chopped, plus a few sprigs to serve
1 whole burrata (about 150g/5½oz)
pinch of ground cumin
salt and freshly ground black pepper

FOR THE DRESSING
½ teaspoon cumin seeds
3 tablespoons olive oil, plus extra to serve
2 tablespoons red wine vinegar
1 tablespoon honey, plus extra to serve
1 teaspoon dried oregano
1 teaspoon garlic purée
1 teaspoon chilli flakes (or to taste)

Toast the sourdough slices, then chop into bite-sized cubes. Tip into a bowl and drizzle with olive oil, then toss in a dry frying pan over a medium heat for a few minutes until golden and crispy. Set aside. These croutons will be the base of the salad, absorbing the dressing and its flavours.

In a salad bowl, combine the tomatoes, olives, onion, cucumber and chopped dill.

To make the dressing, dry-roast the cumin seeds in a small saucepan over a medium heat for 10–15 seconds until fragrant. Tip into a small bowl and add the remaining dressing ingredients. Combine well, then pour over the salad and toss to coat. Season to taste and leave to sit for 10 minutes. During this time, the tomatoes and cucumber will start to release their juices.

Arrange the toasted sourdough on a flat serving dish and pile the salad on top. Add the whole burrata to the top, placing it in the middle of the salad. Garnish with an extra drizzle of olive oil and honey, and a sprinkling of cumin, then serve.

NAANS & FRIENDS

Naan is oven-baked or tawa-cooked/fried bread that is fluffy, soft and delicious. Serve doused in butter or ghee, and use it to mop up curries, wrap around grills or scoop up dips – or as a base for one of my naanizza recipes (see pages 150–151).

In this chapter, I will show you the easiest way to make delicious naans without the faff. You can make any of these breads to go alongside any of the dishes in this book.

PLAIN NAAN

MAKES 4–5

Once you have mastered the art of making naans with my simple recipe and method, you will never buy naans from the shop again. The ingredients can be located readily in all supermarkets, and the dough keeps well in the fridge for up to three days.

300g (10½oz) self-raising flour, plus extra for dusting
1 tablespoon nigella seeds
1½ teaspoons salt
260g (9¼oz/1 cup) Greek-style yoghurt

In a mixing bowl, combine the flour, nigella seeds, salt and yoghurt. Mix with a spoon, then, when it turns crumbly, bring together with your hands to form a dough. Knead for 5 minutes until the dough is soft, elastic and moist, and no residue is left on your fingers. If there is residue, then add a little more flour. Let the dough rest for 5 minutes.

Place a dry frying pan over a medium–high heat to heat up while you roll out the first naan.

Scatter some extra flour into another bowl. Break off a piece of dough about the size of a tennis ball. Roll it into a ball, then press it down into the extra flour. Flip it over and press on the other side.

Dust off the excess and place on the work surface, then use a rolling pin to roll it out into a naan. As you are rolling out the naan, you will notice it springing back; let this happen, then use your hands to stretch it and flip it from side to side to help it stretch to the right size.

Once it is the size of a dinner plate, place the naan in the preheated frying pan and drop 4–5 drops of water on to the edges of the pan – this will create steam to help the naan bubble and rise. Cook on one side for about 2 minutes until it bubbles and browns, then flip to cook on the other side. Keep warm while you roll out and cook the rest of the dough.

PICTURED *Garlic and Coriander Naan (page 149), Chilli-Cheese Naan (page 148).*

SHAPING AND ROLLING OUT THE NAANS

NAANS & FRIENDS

CHILLI-CHEESE NAAN

SERVES 4–5

An easy chilli-cheese naan recipe that is truly addictive – good luck trying not to eat these as you cook!

300g (10½oz) self-raising flour
1 tablespoon nigella seeds
1½ teaspoons salt
260g (9¼oz/1 cup) Greek-style yoghurt

FOR THE CHILLI-CHEESE MIXTURE

1 garlic clove, grated, or 1 teaspoon garlic purée
2–3 tablespoons melted ghee
3 handfuls of grated mozzarella
3 handfuls of grated mature Cheddar
2 tablespoons cream cheese
2–3 green bird's-eye chillies, chopped
½ teaspoon chilli flakes
pinch of sea salt flakes

Combine the chilli-cheese mixture ingredients in a small bowl and keep slightly warmer than room temperature.

In a mixing bowl, combine the flour, nigella seeds, salt and yoghurt. Mix with a spoon, then, when it turns crumbly, bring together with your hands to form a dough. Knead for 5 minutes until the dough is soft, elastic and moist, and no residue is left on your fingers. If there is residue, then add a little more flour. Let the dough rest for 5 minutes.

Place a dry frying pan over a medium–high heat to heat up while you roll out the first naan.

Scatter some extra flour into another bowl. Break off a piece of dough about the size of a tennis ball. Roll it into a ball, then press it down into the extra flour. Flip it over and press on the other side.

Dust off the excess and place on the work surface, then use a rolling pin to roll it out into a naan. As you are rolling out the naan, you will notice it springing back; let this happen, then use your hands to stretch it and flip it from side to side to help it stretch to the right size.

Once it is the size of a dinner plate, place a good handful of the chilli-cheese mixture all around the naan, leaving a 2cm (¾in) border around the edges. Fold the edges of the naan into the middle to create a parcel around the cheese mixture, then shape it into a ball once more before rolling out once again.

Once the naan is the right size, place it in the hot frying pan and drop 4–5 drops of water on to the edges of the pan to create steam. Cook on one side for about 2 minutes until it bubbles and browns, then flip to cook on the other side. Set aside to keep warm while you roll out and cook the rest of the dough.

GARLIC & CORIANDER NAAN

SERVES 4–5

This is a very easy garlic and coriander naan recipe that uses minimal ingredients and is quick to make.

300g (10½oz) self-raising flour, plus extra for dusting
1 tablespoon nigella seeds
1½ teaspoons salt
260g (9¼oz/1 cup) Greek-style yoghurt

FOR THE GARLIC BUTTER
2 garlic cloves, grated, or 1 tablespoon garlic purée
2–3 tablespoons melted ghee
pinch of sea salt flakes
pinch of very finely chopped coriander (cilantro)

To make the garlic butter, mix all the ingredients in a small bowl and keep slightly warmer than room temperature.

In a mixing bowl, combine the flour, nigella seeds, salt and yoghurt. Mix with a spoon, then, when it turns crumbly, bring together with your hands to form a dough. Knead for 5 minutes until the dough is soft, elastic and moist, and no residue is left on your fingers. If there is residue, then add a little more flour. Let the dough rest for 5 minutes.

Place a dry frying pan over a medium–high heat to heat up while you roll out the first naan.

Scatter some extra flour into another bowl. Break off a piece of dough about the size of a tennis ball. Roll it into a ball, then press it down into the extra flour. Flip it over and press on the other side.

Dust off the excess and place on the work surface, then use a rolling pin to roll it out into a naan. As you are rolling out the naan, you will notice it springing back; let this happen, then use your hands to stretch it and flip it from side to side to help it stretch to the right size.

Once it is the size of a dinner plate, place the naan in the preheated frying pan and drop 4–5 drops of water on to the edges of the pan – this will create steam to help the naan bubble and rise. Cook on one side for about 2 minutes until it bubbles and browns, then flip to cook on the other side. Brush with the garlic butter and set aside to keep warm while you roll out and cook the rest of the dough.

NAANS & FRIENDS

CHICKEN TIKKA NAANIZZA

MAKES 4

Rather than ordering pizzas, we love to use naans to create 'naanizzas' at home. They're a great way to use up leftover veg, curries or grilled meats. Here, I've used chunks of chicken tikka and vegetables.

4 Garlic and Coriander Naans (page 149)
1 red onion, finely sliced
2 green bell peppers (capsicums), sliced into strips
200g (7oz) button mushrooms, finely sliced
3 green chillies, finely sliced
4 handfuls of grated mozzarella cheese
4 tablespoons mango chutney (shop-bought)
5 tablespoons Pomegranate Raita (page 162)
handful of chopped coriander (cilantro)

FOR THE CHICKEN TIKKA
400g (14oz) skinless, boneless chicken breasts, chopped into strips
1 tablespoon olive oil
2 tablespoons Greek-style yoghurt
1 tablespoon garlic purée
½ tablespoon ginger purée
2 tablespoons tomato paste (concentrated purée)
1 teaspoon salt
½ teaspoon ground turmeric
1 teaspoon ground cumin
1 tablespoon dried oregano

Preheat the oven to 190°C (375°F/gas mark 5) and line a baking tray with foil or baking parchment.

Combine the chicken tikka ingredients in a bowl and mix so the chicken is evenly coated. Tip into the prepared tray and roast for 20–30 minutes. Once cooked, remove from the oven and set aside, and reduce the oven temperature to 180°C (350°F/gas mark 4).

Arrange the naans on a large baking tray, and sprinkle over a little water to soften them. Divide the chicken tikka between the naans, drizzling over any roasting juices from the tray. Top the naans evenly with the onion, peppers, mushrooms, chillies and cheese, then bake for 3 minutes until the cheese melts.

Remove the naanizzas from the oven and dollop over the mango chutney and raita. Sprinkle over the coriander and enjoy!

MAKES 4

PANEER TIKKA NAANIZZA

This naanizza uses chunks of paneer tikka for a spicy vegetarian treat.

4 Garlic and Coriander Naans (page 149)
1 red onion, finely sliced
2 green bell peppers (capsicums), sliced into strips
200g (7oz) button mushrooms, finely sliced
3 green chillies, finely sliced
4 handfuls of grated mozzarella cheese
50g (1¾oz) canned sweetcorn, drained
24 black olives, stoned and chopped
5 tablespoons Caramelised Garlic Raita (page 167)
handful of chopped coriander (cilantro)

FOR THE PANEER TIKKA
400g (14oz) paneer, cut into cubes
1 tablespoon olive oil
2 tablespoons Greek-style yoghurt
1 tablespoon garlic purée
½ tablespoon ginger purée
2 tablespoons tomato paste (concentrated purée)
1 teaspoon salt
½ teaspoon ground turmeric
1 teaspoon garam masala
1 tablespoon kasoori methi (dried fenugreek leaves)

Preheat the oven to 190°C (375°F/gas mark 5) and line a baking tray with foil or baking parchment.

Combine the paneer tikka ingredients in a bowl and mix so the paneer is evenly coated. Tip into the prepared tray and roast for 20–30 minutes. Once cooked, remove from the oven and set aside, and reduce the oven temperature to 180°C (350°F/gas mark 4).

Arrange the naans on a large baking tray, and sprinkle over a little water to soften them. Divide the paneer tikka between the naans, drizzling over any roasting juices from the tray. Top the naans evenly with the onion, peppers, mushrooms, chillies, cheese, sweetcorn and olives, then bake for 3 minutes until the cheese melts.

Remove the naanizzas from the oven and dollop over the raita. Sprinkle over the coriander and enjoy!

OVERLEAF *Chicken Tikka Naanizza, Paneer Tikka Naanizza, Caramelised Garlic Raita (page 167) and Pomegranate Raita (page 162).*

CHUTNEYS & RAITAS

This may be my favourite chapter in the entire book, as chutneys and raitas can become the star of a dish, enhancing its flavours and making it complete.

At Bindas, all our chutneys are fresh; some of them can last for up to a few weeks in the refrigerator, and some for just a few days. The shorter-life condiments are made up of fresh green herbs like coriander and mint, while the longer-life chutneys tend to have a more involved cooking process, feature spices, and may require cooking down. To make the most of the recipes in this chapter, you will need a good blender or food processor that can blitz the chutneys and raitas to a nice smooth consistency.

GREEN GODDESS CHUTNEY

SERVES 4–6

This is a spicy, creamy, moreish chutney. Pair it with any recipe from Chapters 2 and 5 of this book for a delicious combination.

- 2 large ripe avocados, peeled, stoned and roughly chopped
- handful of coriander (cilantro), roughly chopped (including stalks)
- handful of dill, roughly chopped
- 15g (½oz) parsley, roughly chopped
- 3–6 green chillies (depending on how spicy you like it), chopped
- 5 spring onions (scallions), roughly chopped
- ½ tablespoon ginger purée
- 1 tablespoon garlic purée
- 4 tablespoons extra virgin olive oil
- zest and juice of 4 limes
- 2 tablespoons soft light brown sugar
- 125ml (4fl oz/½ cup) cold water
- generous pinch of salt, or to taste

Simply tip all the ingredients into a blender or food processor and blitz until finely chopped and emulsified. Season to taste, adding more lime juice, salt or sugar if you like.

This will keep for up to 3 days in an airtight container in the refrigerator.

SERVES 4-6

GRILLED PINEAPPLE CHUTNEY

This is more of a chimichurri- or salsa verde-style chutney; it is perfect for dipping, drizzling and dressing, and it offers the perfect combination of sweet and sour, spicy and salty, instantly lifting any dish. You can pair this chutney with any recipe from Chapters 2, 3 and 5 – I personally love to serve it with my Harissa Paneer Tikka (page 120), as well as my Spinach & Leek Pakoras (page 37). Heck, I would even drizzle this chutney on my chips!

300g (10½oz) fresh pineapple, cut into fingers
2 red bell peppers (capsicums), deseeded and halved
2 large red chillies, left whole
2 tablespoons olive oil
2 tablespoons garlic purée
1 tablespoon ginger purée
6 spring onions (scallions), roughly chopped
125ml (4fl oz/½ cup) fresh lime juice
handful of mint leaves, roughly chopped
handful of coriander (cilantro) leaves, roughly chopped
2 tablespoons soft light brown sugar
1 tablespoon dried chilli flakes
1 teaspoon ground cumin
salt

Line a baking tray with foil and preheat the grill to medium.

Arrange the pineapple fingers, red pepper halves and whole red chillies on the prepared tray. Drizzle the olive oil over and season with a pinch of salt. Place the tray under the grill and cook for 6–8 minutes on each side, allowing the fruit and vegetables to blister and char.

Transfer the grilled pineapple, peppers and chilli to your blender. Add the remaining ingredients and blitz until the chutney is well combined. Season to taste with salt.

This will keep for up to 3 days in an airtight container in the refrigerator.

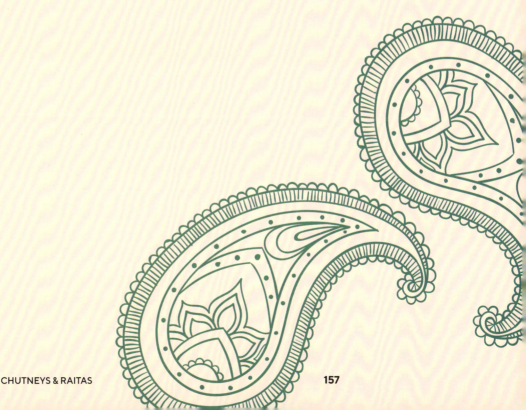

CHUTNEYS & RAITAS

MAMA'S PEANUT CHUTNEY

SERVES 4

This chutney is highly addictive – it should come with a warning. I love to pair it with my Keralan Prawns (page 92) or use it as a salad dressing; I particularly love it with the Beetroot & Chickpea Salad on page 138.

140g (5oz) blanched peanuts
6 garlic cloves, peeled
1 tablespoon olive oil
8 fresh curry leaves
1 teaspoon cumin seeds
1–3 dried red chillies (depending on how spicy you like it)
¼ teaspoon mustard seeds
1 teaspoon chilli powder
1 teaspoon smoked paprika
1 tablespoon maple syrup
1 teaspoon salt
2 tablespoons smooth peanut butter

Heat a dry frying pan over a low heat. Add the peanuts and garlic and toast for 5–6 minutes until golden brown, ensuring they do not burn. Take off the heat and allow to cool for a few minutes.

Heat the oil in a separate frying pan over a medium heat. Add the curry leaves, cumin seeds, dried chillies and mustard seeds, and temper the spices for 10–20 seconds until they pop and sizzle and the aromas are released.

Tip the roasted peanuts and garlic into a blender, along with the tempered spices and their spicy oil. Add all the remaining ingredients and blend briefly to combine. Now add 60ml (2fl oz/¼ cup) water, tablespoon by tablespoon, mixing between additions until you get the right consistency; it should be viscous and flow off the spoon slowly, like liquid velvet.

Once it has reached the right consistency, season to taste and serve.

This will keep for up to 5 days in an airtight container or jar in the refrigerator.

CLOCKWISE FROM LEFT *Green Goddess Chutney (page 156), Mama's Peanut Chutney, Nanima's Tomato Chutney (page 160) and Grilled Pineapple Chutney (page 157).*

NANIMA'S TOMATO CHUTNEY

Nani used to make this chutney all the time; we would eat it with onion pakoras or dollop it on to our tadka daal with steamed basmati rice. The combination of something wholesome and vegan with a spicy, tangy, sweet, juicy chutney is just delicious. Papa liked to eat this chutney with cheese on toast. You can pair it with all your favourite snacks from Chapter 2, or enjoy it with tortilla chips, crispy potatoes, pakoras, burgers and kebabs – the list goes on and on.

5 large vine tomatoes
1 tablespoon olive oil
4 dried red chillies
1 teaspoon fennel seeds
1 tablespoon white vinegar
1 teaspoon caster (superfine) sugar
1 tablespoon garlic purée
½ teaspoon salt
1 teaspoon coarsely ground black pepper

Score two lines all the way around the middle of each tomato, horizontally and vertically, making sure you pierce the skin, but being careful not to cut into the flesh.

Place the tomatoes and 125ml (4fl oz/ ½ cup) water in a saucepan over a high heat. Cook for 5 minutes, then use a pair of tongs or a spoon to carefully rotate the tomatoes so that the tops are now on the bottom. Cook for another 5 minutes.

Once the skins of the tomatoes begin peeling away, remove the tomatoes from the pan using a slotted spoon and carefully remove and discard the skins, then return the peeled tomatoes to the pan with the water. Begin to mash the tomatoes; they will be wonderfully juicy and soft, and perfect for mashing. After another 5 minutes, when the contents of the pan become reminiscent of a good pasta sauce, reduce the heat to low and let it simmer for another 5 minutes. Take the pan off the heat and allow the tomatoes to cool to room temperature.

Meanwhile, it's time to prepare your spices. Heat the olive oil in a small frying pan over a medium heat. Once the oil is hot, add the dried chillies and fennel seeds. Allow them to pop and sizzle, and enjoy the wonderful aniseed aroma that will hit your nose. This will only take 10–15 seconds.

Tip the tempered spices and their oil into a blender, along with the cooled tomatoes and the rest of the ingredients. Blitz on the lowest setting. This is important, as if you do it on a high setting, you are in danger of the spices going bitter.

Season the chutney to taste and serve.

This will keep for 5 days in an airtight container or jar in the refrigerator.

CHILLI GARLIC PESTO

SERVES 4–6

The versatility of Indian spices and Italian herbs is pure magic. This pesto is delicious drizzled over my Burrata with Cumin-Roasted Vegetables (page 52), or as a marinade for any fish, chicken, paneer or potato dish. It is the kind of pesto that can sit in your fridge, ready to be spooned on top of your eggs or smoked salmon on toast, splattered on to roast vegetables or used to breathe life into the protein of your choice. You can even use it as a base for a stir-fried rice if you have leftover rice in the fridge. It is also great with cooked pasta: simply stir it in and serve topped with a healthy measure of Parmesan or Pecorino and a little lemon zest. Try it with my Masala Potato Skins (page 38).

130g (4½oz) unsalted cashews
10 curry leaves
½ teaspoon cumin seeds
large bunch of fresh coriander (cilantro), chopped (including stalks)
30g (1oz) basil leaves
2–3 green chillies
1 teaspoon paprika
4 garlic cloves (add another if you like it more garlicky)
5 tablespoons olive oil
zest and juice of 1 lemon
salt and freshly ground black pepper

Heat a dry frying pan over a low heat. Add the cashews and curry leaves. After 1–2 minutes, as they turn golden, make a well inside the pan and add the cumin seeds. They will pop and cook after 10–15 seconds, releasing a warming herbal aroma. Once you can smell this, allow the cashews, curry leaves and cumin seeds to cool.

Once cool, tip the contents of the pan into a blender and add all the remaining ingredients apart from the lemon juice. Blitz together, then add the lemon juice and blitz again. You want your pesto to be smooth but to still have texture. If you need to add more oil, slowly drizzle it in as you are blending.

Season with salt and a good crack of black pepper to taste. This will keep for up to 5 days in an airtight container in the refrigerator.

FOR A CREAMIER TEXTURE *perhaps to spread on bread or to make a creamy marinade – add 150g (5½oz) mascarpone cheese.*

POMEGRANATE RAITA

I love to serve this pomegranate raita with the Rajasthani Lamb Curry on page 78: it offers the perfect balance of sweetness and tartness, with a hum of garlic and a kiss of spice.

- 100g (3½oz) pomegranate seeds (add more if you wish)
- handful of mint leaves, finely chopped
- handful of coriander (cilantro), chopped
- 1 teaspoon garlic purée
- 1 red chilli, finely chopped
- 350g (12oz) Greek-style yoghurt
- 1 tablespoon olive oil
- zest of 1 lime and ½ teaspoon lime juice
- 1 tablespoon runny honey
- 1 teaspoon ground cumin
- ½ teaspoon chilli powder
- 1 teaspoon coarsely ground black pepper
- 1 teaspoon salt

This is very simple: combine all the ingredients in a mixing bowl and stir everything together, then season to taste and serve!

This will keep for up to 3 days in an airtight container in the refrigerator.

BEETROOT RAITA

SERVES 4

This recipe will soon become one of your favourites: packed with antioxidants, earthy, sweet, spiced and creamy, it is delicious with just about anything. Enjoy this raita as part of a meal, with naan, or with a simple salad.

- 2 cooked beetroots, peeled (I use the ready-boiled ones from the supermarket)
- 1 tablespoon lime juice
- 1 green chilli, finely chopped
- 1 teaspoon garlic purée
- 350g (12oz) Greek-style yoghurt
- 2½ tablespoons runny honey
- handful of very finely chopped coriander (cilantro), leaves picked
- 1 tablespoon olive oil
- 1 teaspoon ground cumin
- 1 teaspoon freshly ground black pepper
- ½ teaspoon chilli powder
- salt

Place the beetroots in a blender, then blend into a purée.

Transfer the beetroot purée to a bowl and add the remaining ingredients. Stir well to combine, season with salt to taste and serve.

This will keep for up to 3 days in an airtight container in the refrigerator.

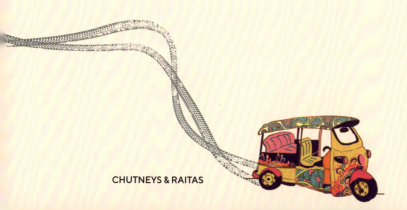

CHUTNEYS & RAITAS

CUCUMBER & MINT RAITA

This classic raita is a go-to recipe that will combine well with any of the dishes in Chapters 4 or 5.

500g (1lb 2oz) Greek-style yoghurt
½ cucumber, shredded or grated (including the skin)
1 green chilli, chopped
1 teaspoon garlic purée (optional)
handful of mint leaves, finely chopped, plus extra to serve
handful of dill, finely chopped (optional)
2 teaspoons caster (superfine) sugar (add more if you prefer a sweeter flavour)
1 teaspoon chilli powder
1 teaspoon ground cumin, plus extra to serve
salt

Combine all the ingredients in a mixing bowl, and season with salt to taste. Serve with a little dusting of ground cumin and some mint for garnish.

This will keep for 2–3 days in an airtight container in the refrigerator. It will release some water during this time due to the cucumber, so its consistency will become thinner, but this will not compromise the flavour.

CLOCKWISE FROM TOP LEFT *Pomegranate Raita (page 162), Cucumber and Mint Raita, Caramelised Garlic Raita (page 167), Apple Raita (page 166), Beetroot Raita (page 163).*

APPLE RAITA

This raita is delicious and cooling, with tart notes from the apple and the freshness of the ginger, mint and yoghurt. I love to serve it on top of a chaat, paired with a spicy curry or as a delicious dip. Sometimes I will use this raita when making my Sweet Potato Chaat (page 40), as the flavour combination of spicy chutney, masala potatoes, sweet, cooling, warming raita and crispy Bombay mix is truly euphoric.

500g (1lb 2oz) Greek-style yoghurt
1 green apple, cored and grated (including the skin)
1 tablespoon ginger purée
handful of mint leaves, finely chopped, plus extra to serve
handful of coriander (cilantro), finely chopped
1 tablespoon runny honey (add more if you prefer a sweeter flavour)
1 teaspoon red chilli powder, plus extra to serve
1 teaspoon ground cumin
1 teaspoon freshly ground black pepper
salt

Combine all the ingredients in a mixing bowl and stir well to combine. Season with salt to taste, then garnish with a little mint on top and a dusting of chilli powder before serving.

This will keep for 2–3 days in an airtight container in the refrigerator.

SERVES 4

CARAMELISED GARLIC RAITA

This raita is highly addictive, and is delicious with anything and everything you serve it with. I would recommend pairing it with any of the dishes in Chapters 4 and 5. Enjoy it over salad, keep it simple and easy with a naan, or devour with poached eggs on toast.

- 6 garlic cloves, whole, skins left on
- 4 spring onions (scallions), finely chopped
- 1 teaspoon cumin seeds
- 1 teaspoon fennel seeds
- 1 teaspoon freshly ground black pepper
- 2 tablespoons olive oil
- 500g (1lb 2oz) Greek-style yoghurt
- handful of mint leaves, chopped
- 1 red chilli, deseeded and finely chopped
- zest and juice of 1 lemon
- 1 tablespoon maple syrup
- ½ teaspoon ground coriander
- salt

Preheat the oven to 165°C (320°F/gas mark 2–3).

Combine the garlic cloves and chopped spring onions in a small roasting tin. Scatter over the cumin seeds, fennel seeds, black pepper and a pinch of salt, then drizzle with the olive oil. Toss to coat, and roast for 20–25 minutes, giving the tin a shake intermittently to move things around.

Once everything has softened and caramelised, remove from the oven and allow to cool. Once cool enough to handle, squeeze the garlic cloves from their skins and add to a mixing bowl, along with the roasted spring onions and the remaining ingredients. Stir to combine and season to taste.

This will keep for up to 3 days in an airtight container in the refrigerator.

CHUTNEYS & RAITAS

DESSERTS & DRINKS

Indians love – and I mean love – desserts! Sweets play a huge role in all our celebrations and are often associated with religious rituals, holding an important place in Indian cuisine and culture.

One reason for this could be the importance of hospitality and generosity in Indian culture. Offering sweets and desserts to guests is seen as a way of expressing hospitality and welcoming them into the home.

During my travels, I have learned that this love of making and sharing sweet treats is a sentiment that is shared globally; wherever you go, sweets inspire pure joy and excitement.

In addition, I have curated a delicious range of cocktails, along with some soul-hugging chai recipes.

CHAIMISU

One of my all-time favourite desserts is tiramisu, but as I live with avid coffee-haters, I decided to turn this delicious Italian dessert into a chai-flavoured version. Here is the result, with Indian spices yet an Italian heart. I call it 'chaimisu'.

300ml (10½fl oz) condensed milk
1 tablespoon caster (superfine) sugar
350g (12oz) mascarpone cheese
4 tablespoons salted caramel sauce (shop-bought)
200ml (7fl oz) double (heavy) cream
30 savoiardi (sponge-cake fingers/ladyfingers)
coconut sugar, for dusting

FOR THE MASALA CHAI
½ teaspoon ground cinnamon
1 cardamom pod
2cm (¾in) piece of fresh ginger
2 black teabags
250ml (9fl oz/1 cup) boiling water

Begin by preparing the masala chai. Combine all the ingredients in a saucepan and bring to the boil. Reduce the heat to low–medium and let it simmer for 8–10 minutes to infuse, then strain the liquid into a bowl and set aside to cool.

Once cooled, add the condensed milk and sugar to the chai, then stir well.

In a separate mixing bowl, combine the mascarpone, salted caramel sauce and double cream. Mix using a spatula until the mixture has a gelato-like consistency.

Arrange half the sponge-cake fingers in a single layer in the bottom of a 21cm (8¼in) square dessert dish. Pour a ladleful of the chai and condensed milk mixture over the top, then add a thick layer of the mascarpone mixture (it should be about 2.5cm/1in thick).

Repeat the process with another layer of sponge-cake fingers, then ladle over the remaining chai mixture and finish with another layer of the mascarpone mixture. Dust it with a little coconut sugar and transfer to the refrigerator for 6–7 hours to set.

Once set, slice and enjoy with a cup of hot masala chai!

CHOCOLATE HALWA

SERVES 4

A firm favourite at the restaurant is our chocolate halwa, a dessert that started life as a delicious experiment and is now one of our bestsellers. I like to serve this halwa with a scoop of vanilla ice cream and some fresh strawberries, with a cup of hot chai or coffee. A warning, however: this dessert is so tasty, it is dangerous.

4 tablespoons ghee
100g (3½oz) fine semolina
2 tablespoons dark cocoa powder
100–150g (3½–5½oz) caster (superfine) sugar (depending on how sweet you like it)
100g (3½oz) milk chocolate chips
375ml (13fl oz/1½ cups) whole milk

Melt the ghee in a saucepan over a medium heat. Once melted, add the semolina and roast for 5–8 minutes until it starts giving off a nice aroma and the colour changes from bright yellow to a warm golden brown. The consistency should be like bubbly wet sand. Stir it constantly so it doesn't catch at the bottom. Add the cocoa powder and 100g (3½oz) of the sugar. Stir well, then reduce the heat to low.

Now add the chocolate chips, followed by the milk, adding a little at a time (you may not need all of the milk, depending on how thick you like it). Using a whisk, continue to stir the halwa, standing back as it will splutter. Keep stirring until it thickens to your desired consistency – I like it to be thick and velvety, but stiff. This will take 2–4 minutes.

Take the halva off the heat and taste to check the sweetness, adding more sugar if required (you do not need to return the pan to the heat; the residual heat will melt the sugar as you stir it in).

Scoop out the halwa into a serving dish and enjoy.

DESSERTS & DRINKS

PISTACHIO KULFI

Kulfi is an Indian ice cream. The beauty of it is that it is so simple to make and does not require churning. For this recipe, you will need popsicle or ice-lolly moulds.

1.5 litres (52fl oz/6 cups) whole milk
50g (1¾oz) caster (superfine) sugar
½ tablespoon candied orange peel
½ teaspoon saffron strands
15g (½oz) shelled pistachios, finely chopped

Pour the milk into a heavy-based saucepan over a medium heat and bring to the boil, whisking it intermittently to prevent it from splitting or burning and to avoid lumps. Once the milk begins to reduce, stir continuously. Once it has reduced by more than half (this will take 15–25 minutes), add the sugar and stir well so it dissolves completely. Next, stir in the candied orange peel, saffron and pistachios, and mix well.

Take off the heat and allow to cool completely, then pour into your lolly moulds. Freeze for at least 24 hours before enjoying.

SAFFRON MILK CAKE

SERVES 6–8

A delicious, crowd-pleasing dessert that is similar to a tres leches cake. Condensed milk kissed with saffron, and soft, moist sponge – it's delicious and decadent. You will need a good stand mixer or an electric whisk for this recipe.

FOR THE CAKE
100g (3½oz) salted butter, softened, plus extra for greasing
½ teaspoon saffron threads
1½ tablespoons hot water
150g (5½oz) self-raising flour
½ teaspoon baking powder
165g (5¾oz) caster (superfine) sugar
3 medium eggs at room temperature
1 teaspoon rose water
1½ teaspoons vanilla bean paste

FOR THE SAFFRON MILK
375ml (13fl oz/1½ cups) whole milk
60ml (2fl oz/¼ cup) double (heavy) cream
120ml (4fl oz/½ cup) condensed milk
pinch of saffron threads

FOR THE TOPPING
375ml (13fl oz/1½ cups) double (heavy) cream
40g (1½oz) icing (confectioners') sugar
handful of dried roses
handful of crushed toffee popcorn (shop-bought; optional)
pinch of saffron threads

Begin by making the cake. Preheat the oven to 170°C (325°F/gas mark 3) and grease a 20cm (8in) square cake tin with butter.

Place the saffron in a small bowl and pour over the hot water. Leave to soak until the water reaches room temperature; the water will turn golden and the saffron will release its scent.

Sift the flour and baking powder into a mixing bowl and set aside.

Add the butter and sugar to a separate mixing bowl or the bowl of your stand mixer. Beat on medium speed until well combined with a velvety, airy texture. Crack in the eggs, then add the rose water, saffron infusion and vanilla. Beat again on medium speed for 1 minute.

Now add the flour and baking powder, and beat on medium speed until you have a smooth, silky batter. Pour this into the prepared tin and bake for 25–30 minutes until a toothpick inserted into the centre of the cake comes out clean.

Remove the cake from the oven and set aside to cool in the tin.

Meanwhile, prepare the saffron milk – the most glorious part of this recipe. Combine all the ingredients in a saucepan, mix well, then place over a medium heat. Bring to the boil, then reduce the heat to low and simmer for 5 minutes.

Take off the heat and leave to cool.

Once the cake and saffron milk have cooled, prick the top of the cake using a fork to make small holes. Pour half of the saffron milk over the cake and let it soak into the airy sponge. Save the rest for later.

Now prepare the cream topping. Combine the double cream and icing sugar in a mixing bowl or the bowl of your stand mixer and beat on medium speed until you have a meringue-like mixture that is aerated and forming peaks. Using a spatula, evenly spread this whipped cream over the cake, then transfer to the refrigerator for a minimum of 5 hours.

When you're ready to serve, slice the cake into squares. Serve in shallow bowls; pour a little of the reserved saffron milk into each bowl, then place a piece of cake on top. Garnish with crushed popcorn, rose petals and saffron, and enjoy.

SERVES 4–6

GINGER CHEESECAKE POTS

If you love cheesecake, you will adore this. White chocolate, buttery biscuits, fiery sweet ginger, and a recipe that is fuss-free and easy to make but looks the part for any occasion. You will need 4–6 individual dessert pots (240ml/8oz) to set the cheesecakes.

FOR THE BISCUIT BASE

200g (7oz) Hobnob biscuits (or oaty cookies)
½ teaspoon fennel seeds
½ teaspoon ginger purée
1 teaspoon ground ginger
100g (3½oz) salted butter

FOR THE CREAM-CHEESE TOPPING

200g (7oz) white chocolate, broken into pieces, plus extra to serve
450g (1lb) full-fat cream cheese
100ml (3½fl oz) double (heavy) cream
1 tablespoon icing (confectioners') sugar, plus extra to serve

TO SERVE

fresh blueberries
sprig of mint

Combine the biscuits, fennel seeds, ginger purée and ground ginger in a food processor and blitz until you have fine breadcrumbs. Melt the butter in a small saucepan over a low heat, then pour this into the food processor and blitz again, this time on a lower setting, until the mixture has been combined.

Take out your individual pots and divide the biscuit mixture evenly between them, gently pressing it into the bases of the pots using the back of a teaspoon.

Melt the white chocolate in a heatproof bowl set over a pan of barely simmering water. Once melted, take the bowl off the heat and add the cream cheese, double cream and icing sugar, stirring with a spatula to combine. Once the mixture is like velvet, spoon the topping into the pots, making sure each pot has the same amount.

Chill for 1–2 hours to set, then top with some grated white chocolate and a dusting of icing sugar. Serve with fresh blueberries and mint.

DESSERTS & DRINKS

HOUSE MASALA CHAI

SERVES 3–4

This is by far the most popular drink we sell at Bindas. Its delicious spice blend is perfect for cold, wintery days, but it's also wonderful on crisp spring mornings, sweltering summer afternoons and in muggy autumn weather. Chai not only lifts your spirits, it also delights your senses and balances your body. The flavour lingers and dances in your mouth, and the aroma of the sweet spices clings to the air. It is the one drink that always instantly makes me feel better and gives me a taste of home.

4–5 green cardamom pods
1 star anise
2 cloves
4 black peppercorns
4cm (1½in) piece of fresh ginger, grated
1 cinnamon stick
1–2 tablespoons loose-leaf black tea, or 2–3 teabags (I would use Assam chai for this)
250ml (9fl oz/1 cup) milk of your choice
soft light brown sugar, caster (superfine) sugar, maple syrup, sweeteners or sugar alternative, to taste

Lightly crush the cardamom pods, star anise, cloves and peppercorns using a pestle and mortar.

Place the crushed spices in a small saucepan and add 625ml (21½fl oz/2½ cups) water. Add the ginger and cinnamon and bring to a simmer over a medium–high heat.

Add the tea or teabags and increase the heat to medium–high. Allow the mixture to bubble for 10 minutes, keeping an eye on it to ensure that it doesn't boil over.

Turn off the heat and allow the tea to steep for 5 minutes, then add the milk of your choice. Stir and bring to a simmer over a medium heat for 6–8 minutes until the tea goes a dark golden brown.

Turn off the heat, then strain through a tea strainer and into a heatproof glass or cup to serve.

Stir in your choice of sugar or sweetener to taste and enjoy.

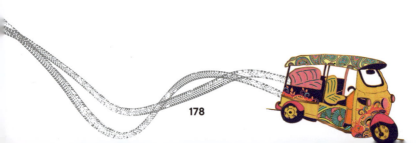

SAFFRON KARAK

Karak is Hindi for 'strong', and this warming drink is a version of chai infused with saffron. The tea is stronger in flavour than masala chai, and the recipe uses fewer spices. The creamy milk, strong tea, spices and aromatic saffron combine to make something really special.

3 teaspoons loose-leaf black tea, or 2–3 teabags (Assam chai is best)
2 cardamom pods
7–8 saffron threads
125ml (4fl oz/½ cup) evaporated milk (this is important, as it will give the chai its signature creamy texture)
caster (superfine) sugar, maple syrup, sweeteners or sugar alternative, to taste

Bring 625ml (21½fl oz/2½ cups) water to the boil in a small saucepan. Once boiling, add the tea or teabags and leave to bubble for 5–6 minutes, then take off the heat and allow to steep for 5 minutes.

Meanwhile, crush the cardamom pods using a pestle and mortar.

Add the crushed cardamom and saffron threads to the steeped tea, then bring to the boil once more. Let it boil for 1 minute, then add the evaporated milk. Bring to the boil once more, then take the pan off the heat and let it sit for 10 seconds.

Now bring it to the boil again, and again take the pan off the heat for 10 seconds.

Repeat this process until the tea goes caramel in colour; it should take about 5–6 rounds of this boiling and resting process.

Strain through a tea strainer into cups, and add your chosen sugar or sweetener to taste.

MAKES 1

QUEEN OF ROSES
GULABI RANI

1 tablespoon rose syrup
4 ice cubes
50ml (1¾fl oz) rose gin
250ml (9fl oz/1 cup) elderflower pressé
pinch of rose petals

Drizzle the rose syrup into a gin glass or tumbler. Add the ice, then pour in the gin. Top up with the elderflower pressé, then garnish with rose petals to serve.

SERVES 4

LYCHEE MOJITO

3–4 lime wedges
5 mint leaves
1½ teaspoons soft light brown sugar
4–5 ice cubes
100ml (3½fl oz) lychee purée
50ml (1½fl oz) white rum
soda water, to top up

Add the lime wedges, mint leaves and sugar to a highball glass. Use a muddler or pestle to muddle them together, squeezing the lime against the bottom of the glass and bruising the mint leaves – but take care not to overdo it.

Add the ice, lychee purée and rum, then use a stirrer to mix the ingredients well. Top up with soda water and serve straight away.

MIRCHI MANGO COOLER

MAKES 1

4–5 ice cubes
1 tablespoon simple syrup
50ml (1¾fl oz) spiced red rum
100ml (3½fl oz) mango purée (shop-bought)
2 teaspoons lime juice
4–6 mint leaves
2–3 slices red chilli
soda water, to top up

Add the ice cubes to a highball glass and drizzle in the simple syrup. Pour in the rum, followed by the mango purée and lime juice. Add the mint leaves and chilli slices, then use a stirrer to mix well and slightly bruise the chillies against the sides of the glass; this will help release their flavour.

Top up with soda water and serve.

SAFFRON SANGRIA

SERVES 6

750ml (26fl oz/3 cups) white wine of your choice (I use a Riesling)
375ml (13fl oz/1½ cups) Prosecco
1 orange, sliced
2 passion fruits, halved
large handful of ice (optional)

FOR THE SAFFRON SYRUP (MAKES 300ML/10FL OZ)

440g (15½oz) caster (superfine) sugar
10 saffron threads
1 teaspoon fennel seeds
2 tablespoons orange zest
1 teaspoon orange extract
pinch of sea salt

Begin by making the saffron syrup. Combine all the ingredients in a small saucepan. Add 250ml (9fl oz/1 cup) water and place the pan over a high heat. Stir well and bring to the boil, then reduce the heat to low and simmer for 3 minutes until it reduces a little.

Take the pan off the heat and allow it to cool. Once the syrup has cooled, transfer into a bottle and refrigerate for at least 1–2 hours before using. (The syrup will keep for up to 2 weeks in the refrigerator, or it can be transferred to a freezer-safe container and frozen for up to 6 months.)

To make the sangria, pour the wine and Prosecco into a large jug. Add saffron syrup to taste (I usually use about 8–9 tablespoons), followed by the orange slices and passion fruit halves. Add ice, if using, and serve.

PICTURED *Mirchi Mango Cooler*

THANK YOU

Thanks will always go to my parents, who taught me to live life without limitations and to pursue what I love.

Special thanks to my best friend Roshni, who has been with me throughout my journey, from concept to fruition, and who always told me that I was destined to cook (and that I had magic hands!). Roshni also taught me to be kinder to myself and to take the wins and losses as life's lessons.

The biggest thanks must go to my husband, who helped me achieve my dreams, took care of all the bills at home, and allowed me the space and freedom to flex my pans. He has always showed belief in me. Throughout this journey, no task has been too big or small, and help was always there when I needed it. We would work 18-hour days, and he was also working full-time as a solicitor. He put his own dreams on the back burner to help me fulfil and achieve my own. Deepak has been my biggest rock, sounding board, best friend and cheerleader. At the start of all this, I had nothing but a dream, a set of pans and three A-boards to my name. Without his selflessness and devotion, I would not have been able to get here.

I would like to thank Martine, my agent, who believed in me and Bindas and who has really championed the food I make.

I would love to take this opportunity to thank my publisher Céline, and the team including Justin, Kristy and Tara, who have worked tirelessly and gone back and forth ensuring that this book captures the heart and essence of what Bindas is and what my food is about. Thank you for allowing me to make my recipes attainable for everyone and for giving them life.

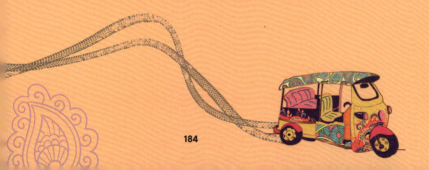

Thank you to Sam, who shot all the glorious images you can see, and to Georgie for designing the mood boards, palette and the whole book. Thank you to Ellie and Alice for making the dishes look so delicious and as perfect as if I made them with my own hands.

I had a lot of fun over the days I was shooting for this book with the whole team; you made the experience seamless and joyful.

Thank you to everyone that has been intrinsic to the journey so far, I hope you use this book to enjoy, relish, celebrate and taste life.

Lastly, thank you to my Bindas brigade: without you, the food cannot be given life and served in our dining rooms.

THANK YOU

INDEX

A
Afghani chicken tikka 116
ajwain seeds 18
    Beetroot & chickpea salad 138
    Chickpea curry 94
    Fish pakoras 36
    Fish tikka 126
    Hot honey garlic prawns 51
    Lamb chop tikka 124
    Masala shakshuka 70
    Mutton curry 108
    Seasonal saag 106
Aloo gobi 102
Apple raita 166
aubergines
    Aubergine bartha 103
    Burrata with cumin-roasted vegetables 52
    Hyderabadi aubergine 86
avocados
    Green goddess chutney 156
    Prawn tikka tacos 46
Ayurveda 18, 19

B
Bang bang sauce 54
beans, green
    Goan chicken & prawn satay 90
beans, kidney
    Daal makhani 81
    Kidney bean curry 95
beetroot
    Beetroot & chickpea salad 138
    Beetroot raita 163
bell peppers *see* peppers

bhaji 19
    Pao bhaji 58
Bombay cheese toast 42
bread and bread rolls
    Cumin Cretan salad 141
    Egg bhurji pao 72
    Lamb & eggs 67
    Pao bhaji 58
    Papa's omelette bun 65
    Potato dumpling pao 66
    see also burgers, naan, toast
broccoli, tenderstem
    Hakka noodles 31
burgers
    Chicken kebab burger 73
    Lamb kebab burger 74
    Paneer tikka burger 63
    Potato chickpea burger 68
    Tandoori chicken burger 60
burrata
    Burrata with cumin-roasted vegetables 52
    Cumin Cretan salad 141
butter chicken 80

C
cake, Saffron milk 176
Caramelised garlic raita 167
carrots
    Beetroot & chickpea salad 138
    Hakka noodles 31
    Pao bhaji 58
    Prawn tikka tacos 46
cashews
    Chilli garlic pesto 161
    Mangalorean chicken 88
    Potato & cashew curry 99

cauliflower
    Aloo gobi 102
    Cauliflower cheese toast 44
    Cauliflower poppers 54
    Masala cauliflower 44
chaat 19
    Sweet potato chaat 40
    Watermelon chaat 28
chai
    Chaimisu 170
    House masala chai 178
    Saffron karak 180
Chapali lamb or chicken kebabs 128
cheese
    Bombay cheese toast 42
    Cauliflower cheese toast 44
    Chaimisu 170
    Chapali lamb or chicken kebabs 128
    Chicken tikka naanizza 150
    Chilli-cheese naan 148
    Lamb kebab burger 74
    Masala potato skins 38
    Paneer tikka naanizza 151
    Papa's omelette bun 65
    Reshmi chicken curry 109
    Tandoori chicken burger 60
    see also burrata, cream cheese, feta, paneer
cheesecake pots, Ginger 177
Chennai 32
chicken
    Afghani chicken tikka 116
    Chapali lamb or chicken kebabs 128
    Chicken kebab burger 73
    Chicken Manchurian 33
    Chicken or paneer makhani 80

Chicken pakoras 34
Chicken tikka naanizza 150
Chipotle chicken tikka tacos 47
Goan chicken & prawn satay curry 90
Kali mirch chicken tikka 122
Lahori karahi chicken tikka 112
Malai chicken tikka 117
Mangalorean chicken 88
Mehak's chicken curry 85
Reshmi chicken curry 109
Simple chicken tikka 114
Sticky chicken 65 32
Tandoori chicken burger 60

chickpeas
Beetroot & chickpea salad 138
Chickpea curry 94
Chickpea masala 68
Hot hummus 26
Potato chickpea burger 68
Roasted chickpeas 26
see also gram flour

Chilli garlic pesto 161
Chilli paneer 45
Chilli-cheese naan 148
chillies, Fried green 66
Chipotle chicken tikka tacos 47
Chipotle salmon tikka 119
Chinese chilli prawns 55
Chocolate halwa 173

chutneys
Green goddess chutney 156
Grilled pineapple chutney 157
Mama's peanut chutney 158
Nanima's tomato chutney 160
Classic kachumber 134

cocktails
Lychee mojito 181

Mirchi mango cooler 182
Queen of roses 181
Saffron sangria 182

coconut milk
Fish moilee 96
Goan chicken & prawn satay curry 90
Hyderabadi aubergine 86
Mangalorean chicken 88

courgettes
Burrata with cumin-roasted vegetables 52

cream cheese
Chicken kebab burger 73
Chilli-cheese naan 148
Ginger cheesecake pots 177
Kali mirch chicken tikka 122
Malai chicken tikka 117
Masala potato skins 38
Masala shakshuka 70
Portobello mushroom tikka 123
Cretan salad, Cumin 141

cucumbers
Chipotle chicken tikka tacos 47
Classic kachumber 134
Cucumber & mint raita 164
Cumin Cretan salad 141
Lamb kebab burger 74
Mango & feta kachumber 134
Paneer tikka burger 63
Sweet potato tabbouleh 136
Tandoori chicken burger 60
Cumin Cretan salad 141

curries
Aloo gobi 102
Chicken or paneer makhani 80
Chickpea curry 94
Daal makhani 81

Fish moilee 96
Goan chicken & prawn satay curry 90
Hyderabadi aubergine 86
Karahi paneer 104
Keralan prawns 92
Kidney bean curry 95
Lahori karahi chicken tikka 112
Lamb & pea curry 100
Mangalorean chicken 88
Mehak's chicken curry 85
Mutton curry 108
Pao bhaji 58
Potato & cashew curry 99
Rajasthani lamb curry 78
Red lentil curry 93
Reshmi chicken curry 109
Seasonal saag 106

D

daal 19
Daal makhani 81
Red lentil curry 93

desserts
Chaimisu 170
Chocolate halwa 173
Ginger cheesecake pots 177
see also cake, kulfi

dill
Beetroot & chickpea salad 138
Cucumber & mint raita 164
Cumin Cretan salad 141
Fish pakoras 36
Fish tikka 126
Green goddess chutney 156
Portobello mushroom tikka 123

drinks
    House masala chai 178
    Saffron karak 180
    see also cocktails

E
eggs
    Egg bhurji pao 72
    Hakka noodles 31
    Lamb & eggs 67
    Masala shakshuka 70
    Papa's omelette bun 65

F
fenugreek, dried *see* kasoori methi
feta
    Beetroot & chickpea salad 138
    Hot hummus 26
    Lamb & eggs 67
    Mango & feta kachumber 134
fish
    Chipotle salmon tikka 119
    Fish moilee 96
    Fish pakoras 36
    Fish tikka 126
Fried green chillies 66

G
garlic 23
    Caramelised garlic raita 167
    Garlic & coriander naan 149
ginger 23
    Chickpea curry 94

Ginger cheesecake pots 177
Lahori karahi chicken tikka 112
Mehak's chicken curry 85
Rajasthani lamb curry 78
Goan-style dishes
    Fish moilee 96
    Goan chicken & prawn satay curry 90
gram flour
    Chicken pakoras 34
    Fish pakoras 36
    Potato dumpling pao 66
    Spinach & leek pakoras 37
Green goddess chutney 156
grilled dishes *see* kebabs, tikka
Grilled pineapple chutney 157

H
Hakka noodles 31
halwa, Chocolate 173
Harissa chapali lamb kebab 50
Harissa paneer tikka 120
herbs 18–19
    see also dill, kasoori methi, mint
Hot honey garlic prawns 51
Hot hummus 26
House masala chai 178
hummus, Hot 26
Hyderabadi aubergine 86

I
ice cream *see* kulfi
Indo-Chinese dishes
    Cauliflower poppers 54

Chicken Manchurian 33
Chilli paneer 45
Chinese chilli prawns 55
Hakka noodles 31
Sticky chicken 65 32

K
kachumber
    Classic kachumber 134
    Mango & feta kachumber 134
kale
    Seasonal saag 106
Kali mirch chicken tikka 122
Karahi paneer 104
kasoori methi 18
    Afghani chicken tikka 116
    Chicken or paneer makhani 80
    Chickpea curry 94
    Fish tikka 126
    Karahi paneer 104
    Malai chicken tikka 117
    Paneer tikka naanizza 151
    Prawn tikka tacos 46
    Tandoori chicken burger 60
kebabs
    Chapali lamb or chicken kebabs 128
    Chicken kebab burger 73
    Lamb kebab burger 74
    Harissa chapali lamb kebab 50
Keralan prawns 92
kidney beans *see* beans
kulfi, Pistachio 174

L

Lahori karahi chicken tikka 112
lamb
    Chapali lamb or chicken kebabs 128
    Harissa chapali lamb kebab 50
    Lamb & eggs 67
    Lamb & pea curry 100
    Lamb chop tikka 124
    Lamb kebab burger 74
    Mutton curry 108
    Rajasthani lamb curry 78
lentils *see* daal
lettuce
    Chicken kebab burger 73
    Lamb kebab burger 74
    Paneer tikka burger 63
    Tandoori chicken burger 60
Lychee mojito 181

M

makhani
    Chicken or paneer makhani 80
    Daal makhani 81
Malai chicken tikka 117
Malaysia 90
Mama's peanut chutney 158
Manchurian sauce 33
Mangalorean chicken 88
mangoes
    Mango & feta kachumber 134
    Mirchi mango cooler 182
masala 19
    Masala cauliflower 44
    Masala mashed potato 42
    Masala potato skins 38

    Masala shakshuka 70
Mehak's chicken curry 85
Mexico 46
mint
    Apple raita 166
    Burrata with cumin-roasted vegetables 52
    Caramelised garlic raita 167
    Chipotle chicken tikka tacos 47
    Cucumber & mint raita 164
    Grilled pineapple chutney 157
    Lahori karahi chicken tikka 112
    Lamb kebab burger 74
    Lychee mojito 181
    Mango & feta kachumber 134
    Mirchi mango cooler 182
    Pomegranate raita 162
    Sweet potato chaat 40
    Sweet potato tabbouleh 136
    Watermelon chaat 28
Mirchi mango cooler 182
mojito, Lychee 181
Mumbai-style dishes
    Bombay cheese toast 42
    Hakka noodles 31
    Lamb & eggs 67
    Pao bhaji 58
    Potato dumpling pao 66
mushrooms
    Chicken tikka naanizza 150
    Masala shakshuka 70
    Paneer tikka naanizza 151
    Portobello mushroom tikka 123
Mutton curry 108

N

naan
    Chilli-cheese naan 148
    Garlic & coriander naan 149
    Plain naan 144
naanizza
    Chicken tikka naanizza 150
    Paneer tikka naanizza 151
Nanima's tomato chutney 160
noodles, Hakka 31

O

omelette, Papa's 65

P

Pakistani-style dishes
    Chapali lamb or chicken kebabs 128
    Harissa chapali lamb kebab 50
    Lahori karahi chicken tikka 112
pakoras
    Chicken pakoras 34
    Fish pakoras 36
    Spinach & leek pakoras 37
paneer
    Chicken or paneer makhani 80
    Chilli paneer 45
    Harissa paneer tikka 120
    Karahi paneer 104
    Paneer tikka burger 63
    Paneer tikka naanizza 151
Pao bhaji 58
Papa's omelette bun 65

peanut chutney, Mama's 158
peas
    Burrata with cumin-roasted vegetables 52
    Lamb & pea curry 100
    Pao bhaji 58
    Potato chickpea burger 68
peppers
    Burrata with cumin-roasted vegetables 52
    Chicken Manchurian 33
    Chicken tikka naanizza 150
    Chilli paneer 45
    Grilled pineapple chutney 157
    Hakka noodles 31
    Harissa paneer tikka 120
    Karahi paneer 104
    Masala shakshuka 70
    Paneer tikka naanizza 151
    Simple chicken tikka 114
pesto, Chilli garlic 161
pineapple chutney, Grilled 157
Pistachio kulfi 174
pizza *see* naanizza
Plain naan 144
pomegranates
    Classic kachumber 134
    Pomegranate raita 162
    Sweet potato chaat 40
    Watermelon chaat 28
Portobello mushroom tikka 123
potatoes
    Aloo gobi 102
    Aloo smash 68
    Bombay cheese toast 42
    Masala mashed potato 42
    Masala potato skins 38
    Mehak's chicken curry 85

Pao bhaji 58
Potato & cashew curry 99
Potato chickpea burger 68
Potato dumpling pao 66
prawns
    Chinese chilli prawns 55
    Goan chicken & prawn satay curry 90
    Hot honey garlic prawns 51
    Keralan prawns 92
    Prawn tikka tacos 46

Q
Queen of roses 181

R
raita
    Apple raita 166
    Beetroot raita 163
    Caramelised garlic raita 167
    Cucumber & mint raita 164
    Pomegranate raita 162
Rajasthani lamb curry 78
Red lentil curry 93
Reshmi chicken curry 109
Roasted chickpeas 26

S
saag 19, 106
saffron
    Saffron karak 180
    Saffron milk cake 176
    Saffron sangria 182

salads
    Beetroot & chickpea salad 138
    Burrata with cumin-roasted vegetables 52
    Cumin Cretan salad 141
    Sweet potato tabbouleh 136
    see also chaat, kachumber
sangria, Saffron 182
Seasonal saag 106
shakshuka, Masala 70
Simple chicken tikka 114
snacks
    Cauliflower poppers 54
    Hot hummus 26
    see also chaat, pakoras, toast
spices 18–19
    see also ajwain seeds
spinach
    Beetroot & chickpea salad 138
    Burrata with cumin-roasted vegetables 52
    Seasonal saag 106
    Spinach & leek pakoras 37
Sticky chicken 65 32
sweet potatoes
    Sweet potato chaat 40
    Sweet potato tabbouleh 136

T
tabbouleh, Sweet potato 136
tacos
    Chipotle chicken tikka tacos 47
    Prawn tikka tacos 46
tamarind
    Chickpea curry 94
    Hyderabadi aubergine 86
    Keralan prawns 92

Mangalorean chicken 88
Tandoori chicken burger 60
tea *see* chai
tikka
    Afghani chicken tikka 116
    Chicken tikka naanizza 150
    Chipotle chicken tikka tacos 47
    Chipotle salmon tikka 119
    Fish tikka 126
    Harissa paneer tikka 120
    Kali mirch chicken tikka 122
    Lahori karahi chicken tikka 112
    Lamb chop tikka 124
    Malai chicken tikka 117
    Paneer tikka burger 63
    Paneer tikka naanizza 151
    Portobello mushroom tikka 123
    Prawn tikka tacos 46
    Simple chicken tikka 114
    Tandoori chicken burger 60

toast
    Bombay cheese toast 42
    Cauliflower cheese toast 44
tomatoes
    Aubergine bartha 103
    Chapali lamb or chicken kebabs 128
    Chicken kebab burger 73
    Chickpea curry 94
    Classic kachumber 134
    Cumin Cretan salad 141
    Egg bhurji pao 72
    Kidney bean curry 95
    Lamb & eggs 67
    Mehak's chicken curry 85
    Nanima's tomato chutney 160
    Paneer tikka burger 63
    Papa's omelette bun 65
    Red lentil curry 93
    Seasonal saag 106
    Sweet potato chaat 40
    Tandoori chicken burger 60

Türkiye 26
turmeric 18

V

vada 66

W

Watermelon chaat 28

Y

yoghurt
    Afghani chicken tikka 116
    Mutton curry 108
    Reshmi chicken curry 109
    see also naan, raita